UNIFIED

UNIFIED

How Our Unlikely Friendship
Gives Us Hope for a Divided Country

SENATOR
TIM SCOTT & TREY GOWDY
CONGRESSMAN

TYNDALE
MOMENTUM®

*The nonfiction imprint of
Tyndale House Publishers, Inc.*

Visit Tyndale online at www.tyndale.com.

Visit Tyndale Momentum online at www.tyndalemomentum.com.

TYNDALE, Tyndale Momentum, and Tyndale's quill logo are registered trademarks of Tyndale House Publishers, Inc. The Tyndale Momentum logo is a trademark of Tyndale House Publishers, Inc. Tyndale Momentum is the nonfiction imprint of Tyndale House Publishers, Inc., Carol Stream, Illinois.

Unified: How Our Unlikely Friendship Gives Us Hope for a Divided Country

Designed by Mark Anthony Lane II

Edited by Dave Lindstedt

Published in association with the literary agency of WordServe Literary Group, www.wordserveliterary.com.

All Scripture quotations, unless otherwise indicated, are taken from the Holy Bible, *New International Version,*® *NIV.*® Copyright © 1973, 1978, 1984, 2011 by Biblica, Inc.® Used by permission. All rights reserved worldwide.

Scripture quotations marked KJV are taken from the *Holy Bible*, King James Version.

Scripture quotations marked NASB are taken from the New American Standard Bible,® copyright © 1960, 1962, 1963, 1968, 1971, 1972, 1973, 1975, 1977, 1995 by The Lockman Foundation. Used by permission.

For information about special discounts for bulk purchases, please contact Tyndale House Publishers at csresponse@tyndale.com, or call 1-800-323-9400.

ISBN 978-1-4964-3041-0

Printed in the United States of America

24 23 22 21 20 19 18
7   6   5   4   3

To Artis Ware, Tim's grandfather, who grew up in a segregated
South and a polarized world, but who learned to love everyone.
His faith and his perspective were transformational.

To Jessie Lee Evans, Trey's grandmother, who shared with
Artis a love for South Carolina and a profound faith in God.

In the segregated age in which they lived, the two never met.
But two generations later, their grandsons became the best of friends.

Here's hoping that Artis and Jessie Lee have met
each other on the other side. May what they now
have in common overwhelm any differences.

Contents

Prologue

June 17, 2015, a day that would become a turning point in our nation's history, began as a typical summer day. In both my hometown of Charleston, South Carolina, and in Washington, DC, where I work, that means hot and sticky. June is one of the least glamorous months in the halls of Congress. The days are long, the work is intense, and there is no downtime as we work to complete our legislative priorities by the Fourth of July. The month is filled with the gyrations, machinations, and frustrations of serving in Congress while important legislation languishes.

There was nothing unusual about that particular Wednesday evening. I had my customary dinner at the Capitol Hill Club—salmon, salad, and iced tea—with fellow South Carolinian Trey Gowdy, who is also my closest friend in Congress. We talked through a number of issues before he went back to his Capitol Hill office and I went to my apartment, where my bedroom had become a make-shift home office. I began making some calls, and I was mid-conversation with someone when I heard the familiar *ping* of call-waiting. When I switched over to take the incoming call, I heard eleven words I will never forget.

"Tim, there's been a shooting in Charleston. It's Clementa Pinckney's church."

Mother Emanuel.

I immediately texted my friends back in Charleston to see what I could find out, but details were scarce. There was an active crime scene with an assailant on the run, but very limited information beyond that.

Soon the details began to unfold: The shooter was white, and the victims were black. The attack was racially moti-vated. The victims were all members of a Wednesday night Bible study. I heard that several people had been killed, but nobody could confirm their identities.

Numb with disbelief, my mind filled with questions that can't be answered this side of heaven. I felt like a ton of bricks had fallen on me, breaking every one of my bones. Everything hurt. I needed to reach out to someone. I needed a friend.

I grabbed my phone and speed-dialed Trey. Given the news coming out of Charleston, a white congressman from the Deep South might seem like an unlikely person for me to call. But I knew he would understand, and I knew he'd be there for me.

TREY

There are times when a phone call can only mean bad news. I had barely returned to my Capitol Hill office after dinner when my cell phone lit up. Tim Scott was calling.

That's curious, I thought. Tim doesn't typically call just to chitchat—not at this hour, and not after we just spent two hours together at dinner.

What could he have possibly forgotten to tell me minutes ago that couldn't wait until morning or couldn't be handled by text?

"Yes, sir," I answered.

"Trey, there's been a shooting in Charleston."

"Where? Who? Why?" When you're trained as a prosecutor, asking questions is the natural first response. It's impossible to get that out of your system, no matter how long you've been out of the courtroom.

"It was Mother Emanuel Church," Tim said. "I know the pastor."

"What happened? Was the shooter apprehended? Do the police have a motive?"

"I don't have all the details, but I know it's bad, Trey. It's really bad."

1

"Welcome to Congress"

Friendship Begins with Trust

TREY

The early days of the 112th Congress felt exciting and occasionally chaotic. Our "freshman orientation" began in late November 2010, after the new members of Congress were elected but before our swearing-in in January. We stayed in a hotel in Washington, DC, and attended meetings, seminars, and panels to learn about the inner workings of government in general and Congress in particular. Current members of Congress taught or facilitated many of the classes, and they offered guidance on everything—including how to structure your office, how to handle travel to and from your district, and how to stay within your office budget.

There were lots of instructions about the procedures governing the floor of the House and all committee work, including strict floor-of-the-House rules about when we could discuss legislative matters, how long we could talk, and even what we could talk about. We had to select an office within one of the three House office buildings and hire the women and men who would work with us in our offices. For those of us who had never served in any legislative body, the learning curve was steep and sometimes confusing.

Congress has its routines, which we would come to know with time and practice, but in those early days, it was all so new. Like walking onto the floor of the House for the first time. Voting for the first time. Getting your member pin and voting card. Seeing your name for the first time on a plaque outside your office.

I will always remember the night our freshman class had dinner in Statuary Hall. I could feel the history. The statues and portraits of yesteryear were all around us. It felt almost as if America's founders were watching and listening. We were walking in the same hallways and meeting in the same rooms where history had been made—and where it would likely be made again.

At the same time, an undercurrent of chaos raced beneath the excitement. Nobody grades on the curve in Congress, and there's not a great deal of margin for those who don't know the ropes, rules, and protocols. Your constituents deserve the same level of representation as those who live in the most senior members' districts, so you must absolutely hit the ground running. You have to assemble staff both in your home district and in Washington. You have to create a plan and a process and a protocol for every conceivable scenario, including how to handle calls for assistance from veterans, seniors, and people seeking passports, as well as calls from those who have insight into particular pieces of legislation. There's a lot to learn, a lot to manage, and a lot to take in.

Orientation is also a time to become acquainted with new colleagues. I needed to get to know the chairs of the committees and subcommittees I was assigned to, as well as their staff members. Women and men whom I had known only from television were now seated a row behind me in a Capitol Hill committee room.

One of my more vivid early memories was stopping by Paul Ryan's office to get his autograph. I'm sure the person who sits out front in his office thought I was crazy. What member of Congress stops by another member's office and asks for an autograph? One that doesn't know any better, that's who!

It seems funny now (and a little ridiculous in hindsight), but Paul had established himself as an ideological leader within our conference, and I wanted him to sign a book for me. He had road maps for tax reform and economic growth, and he was someone many of the freshmen admired and respected. He was, I suppose, famous to me.

Most members of Congress are uncomfortable signing autographs for people, but especially for someone they view as a peer and a colleague. Paul, though, was incredibly gracious and modest about it—as he is about everything. That seems so long ago, and I can't help but smile at the memory—especially since I would later sit next to him on the floor of the House and stop by his office (often bypassing the gate-keeper out front) to try to persuade him to be our Speaker of the House when John Boehner left. And Paul would later ask me to give the nominating speech in front of the Republican Conference when he ultimately ran for Speaker. To go from seeking an autograph to giving a nominating speech is a long, circuitous trip. But in late 2010 and early 2011, everything was new and exciting and unknown—including our famous colleagues.

I also remember meeting fellow freshman congressman Sean Duffy, who is from Wisconsin. In addition to being a reality TV star, a world-class lumberjack, and father to (then) a half-dozen children, Sean was a former prosecutor. At least we had that in common. I met Sean during lunch at one of our first orientation sessions. He was navigating the buf-fet line with his wife, Rachel, and all six of their children. Sean was struggling to hold his infant daughter while mak-ing plates for the other kids, so I offered to take the little girl for him.

"Thank you," he said. "That would be so nice."

"What's her name?" I asked.

He paused, and then said, "I honestly don't remember right now. We have so many."

We both laughed as he handed his daughter over to me and I carried little MariaVictoria through the buffet line.

Thus began my friendship with Sean and Rachel Duffy. As it happened, Sean and I chose our first offices on the same floor of the same building, so we were able to work closely together during our freshman year. Years later, his eldest daughter, Evita, volunteered in my office and did a fantastic job. The friendship that began in that buffet line, with both Sean and Rachel Duffy, has continued to this day.

In the midterm elections of 2010, the Republican Party had captured a majority in the House of Representatives and now had the largest number of Republican members since the late 1940s. Coming just two years into President Obama's first term in office, the arrival of this historically large class of Republicans signaled more than simply a change in control of the House; it felt like the beginning of a significant shift in the balance of power, along with all the attendant responsibilities.

Taking control of the House meant not only a bunch of new members, but also new House leadership and a new legislative agenda. These changes added to the virtual chaos. As the eighty-five freshman Republicans were scrambling to learn the congressional ropes, the newly elevated Republican leadership was scrambling to reassign committee chairmanships, integrate new members into the ongoing work of the House, and install their own priorities and agenda. The leaders within the Republican Conference in the House had been anticipating and preparing for the potential chance to govern, and now the moment had arrived. It was time to actually start. The political calculus in the Capitol had been altered, and the town was buzzing with curiosity.

The new roster for the 112th Congress involved an interesting cast of characters, including veterans of the Iraq War, a former NFL player, Ivy League graduates, police officers, farmers, a representative who would later become director of the CIA, and several others who would quickly move up to the US Senate. In the middle of all that were four new Republicans from South Carolina—Jeff Duncan, Mick Mulvaney, me, and Tim Scott, the first African American Republican congressman elected from our state since George W. Murray in 1896. We captured some attention, in large part because there were four of us, and some in the media dubbed us "the Four Horsemen." Tim and fellow freshman Allen West of Florida were the first black Republicans elected to the US House since J. C. Watts of Oklahoma retired in 2003—making them veritable unicorns on the political scene.

Though the 2010 freshman class certainly made news as a whole, having a black Republican from South Carolina representing the very district where the Civil War began was especially noteworthy. Tim had already become a historically significant figure in South Carolina, as he continues to be. He was a man of color elected over a host of alternatives, including two sons of beloved political figures in our state. To get to Washington, Tim had emerged from a crowded primary field that included Paul Thurmond, the son of legendary senator Strom Thurmond, and Carroll Campbell III, the son of an immensely popular former congressman and governor. He then handily defeated his Democratic opponent in the general election.

Tim also made everything look very, very easy. Meeting new people seemed easy for him. Understanding the legislative process seemed easy for him. Building his office staff seemed easy for him. Even appearing on television seemed easy for him. He never seemed like a "true freshman" as the rest of us did. It appeared as if he had been serving in Congress for decades. I hadn't met him before we started orientation together, but he seemed warm and approachable, though perhaps ever-so-slightly guarded. I would soon learn that his guardedness was a carefully honed defense mechanism, developed through many years of experience. Tim's skill set, coupled with his infectious personality, brought instant notoriety and a steady stream of requests for his time and attention. House Republican leaders not only *knew* about Tim Scott, they wanted to make him the face of the "new Republican Party."

With eighty-five new Republican representatives in town, which included a gain of sixty-five seats in the House, the competition for committee assignments and media attention was fierce, as you can imagine. The freshmen were jockeying for position, looking for places to shine, and hoping for media appearances. Television is such a powerful force, and media interviews were highly coveted for most freshman members. Many people, both in Washington and back home in our districts, equated being seen with being relevant. In our line of work, when the world sees you on television, you have some stature. Whether that is fair, or as it should be, is certainly open to debate. But the power of the screen is not.

As I am fond of saying (only a little bit facetiously), "With the possible exception of love, TV is the most powerful force on the planet."

Committees are a big deal in Congress, and new members are integrated into the work of the House through their committee assignments. Getting on the right committee is almost essential to your ability to effectively legislate in your area of expertise or interest. The challenge is this: The newest members have the least seniority, they don't always get their preferred committee or subcommittee requests, and they are the last to speak in committee hearings. By the time your turn comes, all the good questions have usually already been asked. You have to be very creative, and you only have five minutes to ask new questions or follow up on your colleagues' previous questions. How well can you distinguish yourself in five minutes, after all the good material has been taken and discussed? It isn't easy.

Early on, I learned how important it is to prepare for committee hearings: Read the materials, do your own independent research, and use your five minutes of questioning as well as you can. I looked for a line of questioning that was different or unique. I showed up on time, and I listened to my colleagues who had been doing this for a long time. Mike Pence, Jim Sensenbrenner, Dan Lungren, Randy Forbes, Bobby Scott, and several others were seasoned questioners. I watched them closely, and I tried to learn.

Your committee assignments control most of your time, allow you to pursue your policy objectives, and often dictate your sphere of influence. If you're an attorney who wants to reform the civil or criminal justice systems, for example, it is essential to be on the Judiciary Committee. If tax reform is your calling, you need to be on the Ways and Means Committee.

These highly significant committee assignments are made by the House Steering Committee, which sometimes seems as if it is populated by Zeus, Poseidon, the Titans, and the Cardinals. The Steering Committee sits behind closed doors and not only picks committee chairpersons, but also fills all the other committee slots. The most highly coveted committees in the House—Ways and Means, Energy and Commerce, Appropriations, and Rules—get people like Tim Scott. Then the committee gods look at who's left—someone like me, for example—and they think, *Well, we have to put him somewhere, don't we?*

Because I was a former prosecutor, the Judiciary Committee seemed like a natural fit for me. Former Majority Leader Eric Cantor and then–Judiciary Committee chairman Lamar Smith were very instrumental in making that happen. Had Eric and Lamar not taken a chance on me, I would never have been on the Judiciary Committee. I also was placed on the Committee on Oversight and Government Reform, thanks to Darrell Issa, and the Committee on Education and the Workforce, which was a committee near and dear to the heart of former House Speaker John Boehner.

Tim was initially placed on the Small Business Committee and the Transportation and Infrastructure Committee, but he later relinquished those appointments when he was selected by Speaker Boehner for the powerful House Rules Committee. The House Rules Committee determines the order of business in the House, which amendments are made and in what order, and how bills will be brought to the floor. Tim's appointment to the Rules Committee was a testimony to his obvious talents as a legislator, as well as an indication of his rapid rise to significance in the House. It was just one more example of the superstar status Tim achieved right from the start.

TIM

Though Trey and I are both from South Carolina, a relatively small state, we had never met before our election to Congress. I remember the first time I met Trey at freshman orientation. From the beginning, he struck me as someone who is sharp, clear, and articulate. To win a congressional seat, Trey had to defeat an incumbent Republican congressman, which is no small feat. You have to be tenacious, and you have to be disciplined. Trey Gowdy is both of those things.

One of Trey's signatures is his wardrobe. His suits are not flashy, but they're . . . well, unusual. His appearance is always interesting, from his hair to his shoes, including his socks. (He has been known to wear a dark suit with white socks.) When you first meet him, he seems fairly understated; but if you engage him in conversation, you very quickly realize that first impressions can be misleading.

Though Mick Mulvaney, Jeff Duncan, and I had previously served in the South Carolina legislature, Trey's background was as a prosecutor with several appearances on *Court TV* and *Forensic Files*. It had to have been difficult to come into Congress without any prior legislative experience, but Trey is a quick study and a disciplined student. His acumen as a prosecutor was well known in South Carolina, and it wouldn't be long before the nation would discover that Trey has a very special gift for cross-examination.

As we acclimated to Congress, the four of us started meeting to confer on the issues and discuss how we were leaning on upcoming votes. We were motivated by the need to get up to speed quickly, and we were all looking for ways to be as prepared as possible for the task at hand. We ate dinner together as often as we could, and we would bounce ideas off each other and take advantage of our different perspectives, passions, experience, and expertise.

A lot of folks in our incoming class were in a similar age range, significantly younger than the average member of Congress. With all that youth came inexperience, but also optimism. We were motivated by the challenge of serving the nation.

We had some great mentors in the other two members of our state delegation, Joe Wilson and Jim Clyburn. We called Joe Wilson our scoutmaster. He's about fifteen years older than we are, and he was our senior member of Congress on the Republican side. He did everything he could to help us get into the rhythm of our committee assignments. Joe is full of optimism and always has a word of encouragement for us. He is among the most thoughtful and considerate people in the House.

Similarly, Democrat James Clyburn became a strong ally on all things pertaining to South Carolina. Though he is on the other side of the aisle, he was kind and gracious to us from the day we arrived. Well respected as a senior statesman, Mr. Clyburn has always been dedicated to the progress of South Carolina and the nation. We appreciated that we could always turn to him for help with state projects and to advocate with our colleagues on both sides of the aisle. Even now, he is highly respected for his knowledge on a number of issues as well as his influence as a member of the Democratic leadership.

TREY

During freshman orientation, while the rest of us were trying to figure out where lunch would be served, Tim was already interviewing potential staff members. Seriously, he once left an orientation lunch to interview potential legislative directors in the lobby of the hotel. He hit the ground running, analyzing which roles to seek on which committees far more strategically than the rest of us.

When you're new to DC, the most enviable position is in the eye of the media, and Tim had daily opportunities for TV appearances. He was gracious, and he always had time for Mick, Jeff, and me, but he was light-years ahead of us in terms of exposure, prestige, and notoriety. The rest of us were never asked to go on television to discuss the issues, because nobody knew who we were. It wasn't the media's fault; they simply had never heard of Mick Mulvaney, Jeff Duncan, or Trey Gowdy. Nobody scrutinized our affiliations, as they did when Tim chose not to join the Congressional Black Caucus. No one in the media asked whether the white conservative Republican congressmen from South Carolina would be able to connect with the first black president of the United States. All of that was reserved exclusively for Tim Scott. He had a perch that the rest of us could not attain. With it came pressures the rest of us could barely imagine.

I remember sitting one night with Tim, Jeff, and Mick in a DC restaurant, early in January 2011, when Tim politely excused himself to, as he said, "honor a prior commitment." As he rose from the table, he smiled a smile that I've since learned means he knows something the rest of us don't know. Twenty minutes later, I glanced up at a large-screen TV in the dining room, and there was Tim Scott, larger than life, being interviewed on national television. But Tim wasn't touting his own importance. He never even told us where he was going. He was almost embarrassed by the fact that he was famous. But he was, and fame comes with a cost.

I, on the other hand, was one of the least known members of our freshman class—and for many good reasons. There was nothing particularly special about my arrival in Washington, except to my mom. Middle-aged, gray-haired men with law degrees are a dime a dozen on our side of the aisle. I had never served in the South Carolina state legislature. I had never been anything other than a prosecutor—no county council, no school board, and no legislative branch experience.

I got to Congress by winning the Republican primary against an incumbent congressman, which is hardly the way to ingratiate yourself to others in the party. The media labeled me as part of the Tea Party movement, mostly because it was the easiest way to explain how I had won; but it was also because they viewed that label as a pejorative. But in actuality, no Tea Party group supported me in the GOP primary. The Tea Party supported my friend and fellow candidate Jim Lee. I wasn't anybody's favorite. I hadn't ever met John Boehner, Eric Cantor, or Kevin McCarthy before the 2010 Republican primary. So when I arrived in Washington after the election, there were few, if any, expectations for me beyond the lines of my district, and there was no spotlight seeking me out.

Riding into town with Tim Scott, the new hero of the Republican party, I knew I had a choice. I could mind my own business and try to figure things out for myself. I could be jealous of his fame and notoriety (which is a popular option in our line of work). Or I could ask myself some questions about this rising star from Charleston, South Carolina.

How did he get here?

What are the qualities that put him in this position?

How is it that he is always gregarious, always in a good mood, and always humble?

I watched him, and I took mental notes.

Tim could have easily won the job of freshman class president, except he didn't run for it. We tried to get him to run. He would have been the only candidate if he had run. No one would have challenged him. But he didn't run.

(Mental note: This guy has some humility.)

He could have dominated every freshman class meeting. We actually wanted him to talk more! But he spoke only when he believed he had something of real importance and significance to add.

(Mental note: This guy knows when to speak and when to listen.)

He could have had whatever position and any committee assignments he wanted in that Congress, but he opted for a behind-the-scenes role where he would have influence even if no one else knew it.

(Mental note: This guy is strategic.)

I was intrigued by this up-and-coming colleague with unmistakable star power who seemed to break all the clichés and conventions of chasing the spotlight. Tim was a shining light in the epicenter of the political world, he was in constant demand from the media, and he had a cadre of young black conservatives seeking him as their mentor. And he was in the midst of a meteoric rise to prominence on one of the largest stages in American government. A confluence of factors like these would cause a lesser man to change his personality in a town fully capable of distorting one's perspective. But none of this changed a single thing about Tim

Scott. From the very beginning, I knew one thing for sure: This man was different. He was at peace with who he was, and he wasn't going to change.

One of the things that made Tim unique was his understanding of the difference between perceived power and real influence. You might assume that pursuing the most visible position he could obtain would be the ticket to success, but that's not how it worked out. Instead of running for freshman class president, Tim took a job with the Elected Leadership Committee, a behind-the-scenes role that required him to advocate on behalf of the other freshmen.

The ELC is an in-house committee that works closely with the Speaker of the House, the Majority Leader, the Majority Whip, the Chairman of the Republican Conference, and the Assistant Chairman to decide the party's strategy and direction for the weeks and months to come. Our freshman class was so large that one out of every three Republican representatives was new to Washington. Someone needed to be the conduit, the bridge, to take our ideas back to leadership. Virtually no one in South Carolina would have chosen this low-profile role for Tim. No political adviser would have possibly recommended this role. "Be the class president!" That is what the experts would have advised. The only people who appreciated his decision to represent us on the ELC were the eighty-four other freshman Republicans who needed a powerful advocate at the leadership table. Tim opted for a less-visible position—unseen by voters, the media, and the world—in order to make a difference on issues that really mattered and reflected who he was at his core. No one does that. Except Tim Scott.

Because I had no previous legislative experience—or any experience other than in a courtroom—I really needed someone I could go to quietly and say, "What's happening now? What's going on? What happens next? And why?" I needed someone who wasn't trying to compete with me and who wouldn't use my lack of experience against me. In short, I needed a colleague I could confide in and trust, and I needed that person in a profession that's not always known for rewarding trust and confession.

While I developed a close relationship with all three of the guys I came with to Washington from South Carolina, I was particularly drawn to Tim's humble and open personality. And just as Elvis Presley wasn't threatened by a stagehand or the guy who plugged in his amplifier, I was no threat to Tim Scott at all. Still, I knew it was rare to find someone who would say, "Sure, I'll help you, and I won't tell everyone you need it."

I realized early on there wasn't much I could do to pattern myself exactly after Tim. I cannot change the way I look. I don't have a beautiful bald head or an engaging smile that draws the world in. But I could spend some time with him, as much as his schedule would allow, and I could find out what he had learned about how to succeed in Congress.

The Four Horsemen from South Carolina have a unique relationship with each other, and Mick Mulvaney and Jeff Duncan have always been very helpful to both Tim and me, but as time went on in those early days, it became increasingly difficult to align all four of our schedules. Jeff began meeting more often with a group we called the Cajun Caucus, led by our dear friend Congressman Jeff Landry, who is now attorney general for the state of Louisiana; and Mick began to form and meet with a group that over the course of time would become the House Freedom Caucus. Increasingly, it was just Tim and me at dinner. Because we're both introverts, we're very comfortable relating one-on-one or in a small group. We quickly discovered our mutual love for the Dallas Cowboys and South Carolina Gamecocks. (Some seasons, pulling for Dallas and South Carolina could be a lonely pursuit.)

Tim and I are both nondrinkers and non-partiers, so our dinner plans and availability seemed to match up well. We now make a conscious decision to save the dinner hour for each other, but it didn't necessarily begin that way. At first, it was a dinner every so often. Then it went to once a week, and eventually it became our highest priority. Our table was never closed. Mick would stop by many nights—as he still does from time to time, even though he is no longer in the House—but most nights it was Tim and me.

Our friendship was not just over food. We also began to collaborate on work issues. One of the first times I can remember working directly with Tim was when he and I ended up on the same side of the vote to reauthorize the Export-Import Bank, which was a big issue in South Carolina. Mick and Jeff were voting the other way, which meant we were split 2–2.

We were a pretty tight delegation, so that was unusual for us. Because South Carolina is a small state, it was important for the four of us to sync our watches. If we split 2–2, it meant to some people back home that two of us were wrong. We needed to be prepared to explain not only our own votes, but also why we had split—and all without criticizing the two who voted differently. Tim and I felt comfortable enough with each other, and trusted each other enough, to effectively explain why we voted the way we did.

For me, our friendship took a dramatic turn one evening when Tim showed up to the table looking overwhelmed and perplexed, which was odd. I'd never seen him anything less than fully composed and fully in control. When I asked if there was anything I could do, anything he needed, he shared with me the darker side of being politically sought after. Turned out, there actually were some frustrations with living in the spotlight, being everything the rest of the world wanted him to be. Tim was famous, in demand, constantly sought out. He was also exhausted—both physically and emotionally.

As he still does at times today, he was trying to say yes to everyone and everything, and he was being pulled in a thousand directions. Colleagues were asking him to get involved in nearly every major legislative initiative, and he was struggling to say no. On that night, and for just a moment, he seemed vulnerable. He seemed mortal. He seemed to be in need of some trusted counsel and a friend who would simply listen.

TIM

As our schedules filled up and our committee assignments began to demand more of our attention, the Four Horsemen remained intentional about our time together. Jeff Duncan and I shared an apartment, and we became close friends. Trey and Mick knew each other from back home, and they continued to spend time together. The four of us still had dinner together often, as well as several collective media interviews.

But at some point, as usually happens in any relationship, the competing demands on our time began to pull us away from one another. Soon, it became just Trey and me at the dinner table, more often than not. It wasn't planned at the beginning; it just happened organically. He and I began to develop our own friendship, and we began to appreciate the role we could play in each other's lives, both in Washington and at home.

It didn't take long for me to become aware of the media's high interest in the two new black Republicans, Allen West and me. The Republican House leadership encouraged us to be as visible as we felt comfortable with on the issues that mattered to each of us. It was an incredible opportunity for them to have two African American Republican members of Congress. The demands were intense. I had total autonomy to decide how involved or uninvolved I wanted to be, but the volume of media requests was constant—and often through the roof.

I quickly decided that I did not want to become the guy

who represents "the conservative black perspective" on every issue. Allen and I both wanted to find our own stride, determine our own answers to the issues, and just be ourselves in the political climate. Yet I wanted to answer enough of the questions and respond to enough of the interviews that my voice would be heard where it could possibly make a difference. This created a tension that began to take its toll. With such a steady stream—or torrent—of opportunities, it was difficult to decide which interviews to take and which to decline. No matter how many times I said yes, I was still turning down 95 percent of the requests.

Trey brought so much truth to that dilemma. He always encouraged me to guard the brand I had created. Trey is very purposeful, and he reminds me to be that way as well. He told me that I did not have to accept the requests and assignments that were not in my best interest. He was very sensitive to the reality of politics and race, and he knew that while it might be helpful to the party to have a black Republican speak out on any number of issues, it might not be helpful to me as an individual.

I'll never forget Trey's advice that evening when I was feeling exhausted. In a lot of ways, it cemented our friendship and set a pattern for how we would speak into each other's lives as friends. He said, "Tim, you worked your tail off to get here. No one up here endured what you did to get elected to the US House. You challenged a highly competitive field in a primary, and almost nobody up here was knocking on doors in the Charleston heat to get those votes. You have earned every bit of the political capital you have. Don't let others spend it. Don't take on every issue simply because it is better for the party to have you as a spokesperson. Don't let other people use your political capital, unless you decide you want to. You decide if, when, and where to spend it."

That was exactly what I needed to hear.

TREY

From a personal standpoint, what Tim really needed was someone he could trust, someone who would listen to him, someone who could possibly understand what he was going through, even if I had not experienced it myself. From a practical standpoint, all he really needed was some help prioritizing his time. On top of that, he just needed to be reminded that he had *earned* everything that had come to him—and it was therefore *his* to invest, conserve, and employ.

After that conversation, I remember thinking, *I have finally contributed something to this guy who, a week ago, I didn't think needed anything. He seemed to have everything.* (Then again, we know that no one truly has everything, regardless of appearances.)

Here's the moral of the story, for me: I don't care how great things may *appear* to be going in someone else's life; we *all* need somebody we can trust, that we can be fully candid with, and who will give us the best advice for *us* and not just for *them*. I have certainly benefited from others giving me their unconditional affirmation and encouragement, and their counsel without an agenda, and this was a chance for me to pay it forward to someone else. Of course, it was helpful to the Republican Party to have a mosaic of faces to present to the public. There is certainly a benefit to the synergy of representatives such as Tim Scott, Mia Love, Elise Stefanik, Marco Rubio, and Will Hurd. But the question was not what was best for the Republican Party or even for me. The question was what was best for Tim Scott. I reminded him of the path he had traveled to get where he was, and we reflected on the loneliness of running for office.

I also passed along to Tim some advice I had received from Paul Ryan: "Find what you're good at, and do more of it. Find what you're bad at, and stop doing it." It's not quite Aristotle or Kierkegaard, but Paul's counsel was eminently wise and practical—and much easier to remember. I also shared some advice I'd received from David Wilkins, former speaker of the South Carolina House and US ambassador to Canada under George W. Bush. Wilkins had once told me, "It's better to be a good guy with a bad idea than a bad guy with a good idea."

I synthesized the wisdom of Paul Ryan's and David Wilkins's advice into my own personal mantra: "Find what you're good at, and be a decent person in the process."

Tim and I were in completely different spots. He was the most famous and most influential member of the historic freshman class of 2010, while I was a virtual unknown to anyone except for my family and friends. But I thought the Ryan/Wilkins mantra could possibly work for both of us.

In that conversation, we began to forge a friendship of the rarest kind in politics: one devoid of pretense. In our line of work, most relationships are transactional. In other words, "What's in it for *me*? What do I stand to gain from this?" Relationships where people put the other person first and remain committed to giving their best counsel for the benefit of the other person are few and far between.

The conversation that changed the tenor of our relationship began innocuously enough. Tim and I had certainly been friendly before that, but when the most popular and respected new member of Congress was vulnerable enough to risk asking for help, it showed that even the best and the brightest can have moments of doubt and indecision. In the world of politics, where people too often exploit others' perceived weaknesses and attempt to gain advantage through any means, Tim's willingness to let down his guard was different and remarkable. Though I didn't think about it at the time, my willingness to offer my best counsel, rather than looking for an angle to advance my own interests, was probably different too. Knowledge is power in politics, and keeping the vulnerable confidence of a fellow elected official is rare. There are times when sharing knowledge will benefit only the one who has exposed the shared vulnerability. Integrity means keeping the confidence. That isn't politics. That is friendship. Friendship trumps politics. Or at least it should.

As a result of that conversation, Tim and I began to build trust with one another, and that has increased exponentially over the course of our time in Congress. Once you know someone will keep a confidence, give you sound counsel, and genuinely have your best interests at heart, there is no limit to what you can share, and there is no limit to what can be gained. Today, even the national media reporters recognize there is something different about our friendship. They don't refer to us as colleagues or delegation mates; they refer to us as close friends. This friendship that began because of politics is hardly constrained by politics. Our connection is emotional and spiritual and real, and it affects every facet of our lives—from sharing our deepest fears and frustrations to calling each other's mom on her birthday.

In 2014, there was a prominent sticker on the back of my mother's car: *Tim Scott for Senate*. In my opinion, it was displayed even more conspicuously than her *Trey Gowdy for Congress* sticker. (Not that I would notice or carry a grudge.) Of course, she wanted us both to win. But I think what she really wanted was for people in Upstate South Carolina to know she was pulling for a young man from Charleston who was like a brother to her own son. This year, the flowers Tim sent my mom on her birthday arrived before the ones I sent. Do not ask me why or how that happened! But because Tim not only remembers my mom's birthday but actually does something to celebrate it, I suspect that *Tim Scott for Senate* sticker will probably stay right where it is.

Our trust and friendship have grown, and we've made room at the table for others, as well. At our nightly meals, we're almost always joined by new friends who have entered our lives from both sides of the aisle. We have shared many meals with Tom and Anna Cotton and their children, Marco and Jeanette Rubio and their children, Lindsey Graham, Joni Ernst, Stacey Plaskett, Tulsi Gabbard, Luis Gutiérrez, Peter Welch, John Ratcliffe, Jason Chaffetz, Mia Love, Mark Walker, and too many others to recall. It's a fascinating experience to have such a diverse group of friends sharing a meal together. That table is big enough for all people of good conscience, across any line you can imagine.

TIM

Though Trey and I bonded over things we have in common, there was a time in our state's history when our friendship would have been impossible. My mother, Frances Scott, would have been delighted to imagine the beauty of this friendship, but segregated schools, water fountains, and restaurants were the norm in her generation. Even at the time I was born, segregation was more typical than not in the South. My mother's generation knew a very different South than the one in which Trey and I would come of age. I cannot fathom the shock and amazement that our unlikely friendship would have sparked when we were kids.

In so many ways, we are two very different people. I'm a big-picture person, and I like to focus on vision. Trey is more analytical and strategic. He remembers everything that ever happened. Others have told me my memory is very good, but I don't necessarily agree. I try to have a *selective* memory: I choose not to remember the negative. It's actually a pretty effective strategy. I lead with hope; Trey is more of a skeptic. He thinks well on his feet and is an expert at cross-examination; I tend to analyze things later. He's a fantastic student, and his preparation is impeccable. I enjoy assessing and planning, but he enjoys dissecting. I've worked hard to excel, but Trey is naturally brilliant. Because of our different backgrounds and life experiences, there are times when our vantage points are polar opposites. But one thing that binds us together is a true desire to know each other beyond our differences. We utilize that knowledge and our different perspectives to make each other better.

One of the keys to overcoming problems in our society is finding common ground. We don't have to agree on *everything*, but wherever we *do* agree . . . let's start there. I have found commonality to be a powerful tool. Trey understands the concept of mutually beneficial opportunities as well as anyone I've ever met, especially in leadership. His lifestyle reflects what we're talking about. One of the reasons Trey and I have been able to have some frank discussions about problems, challenges, and obstacles—and overcome them very quickly—is that we have intentionally sought to find common ground. No matter what differences we may have with another person—social, racial, political, spiritual, ideological—if we will look for *something* we have in common, or something we can admire or emulate in the other person, we can always build on that.

Trey and I are both in politics, but politics is not going

to change the nation. We will change the nation only by changing the condition of the human heart. And that can only happen through love. True friendship is born out of acceptance and unconditional love—a love that is consistent and intentional.

I'm very optimistic about our future, but if we're going to change the world, it will happen through friendship. It will happen as each of us enlarges our comfort zone to make room for unlikely friendships with people with whom it may appear, at first glance, we have little in common. Pursuing unlikely friendships will require us to do things that seem uncomfortable at first. But what is hard becomes easier with practice. As we choose to do the hard things, we will soon reap the benefits.

2

Tested by Success

The Call to the Senate

TREY

In politics, conventional wisdom says that you should always reach for the highest rung you can grasp. There is an implicit pressure to move up. If you have an opportunity for an office or a promotion or a title, you should always, always, always take it. It's kind of the number one rule. You always want to make the people back home proud. You want your voters to be able to say, "Look at our guy, doing so well."

Toward the end of 2012, I received a brief but surprising phone call. I was sitting in the parking lot at the Country Club of Spartanburg, having just picked up a Christmas gift for my father, when Senator Jim DeMint called to let me know he was leaving the US Senate. He had been reelected to a second six-year term in 2010, but he had decided to assume a leadership position at a conservative think tank.

Senator DeMint's resignation created a rare open seat in the US Senate for South Carolina. Strom Thurmond had represented our state for nearly fifty years, and Ernest Hollings had served for nearly forty. Senator Hollings was one of the longest-serving senators in our nation's history, yet he was the *junior* senator from South Carolina until his final two years in office. Suffice it to say, Senate seats did not come open very often in South Carolina.

Jim DeMint had not served nearly as long as Senator Thurmond or Senator Hollings, but for many of us, he was the gold standard for conservatism and would be a hard act to follow. He cast a long shadow in South Carolina politics, and his replacement was sure to receive a lot of scrutiny, both locally and nationally. In our short conversation, Senator DeMint was genial and humble as always, and he wished me well.

It doesn't take long for people in our line of work to process information like a soon-to-be-vacant seat in the Senate.

Hmm. There's an opening in the United States Senate. I wonder how that gets filled . . . ?

In our state, the governor appoints a temporary replacement until the next general election. In this case, Republican Nikki Haley (now ambassador to the United Nations) had a unique opportunity to make a decision that could affect the representation of our state for a long time. It made sense that she would consider current members of the House of Representatives, among others, to fill that slot.

As soon as I hung up from talking with Senator DeMint, my next call was to Tim Scott. While he and I were on the phone, Mick Mulvaney called. There was an opening in the US Senate, and we were all wondering what would happen next.

TIM

When Senator DeMint called to inform me of his intentions, my first response was to ask him to reconsider. He's a good man with a tremendous impact, and I hated to see him leave. However, he said he had an opportunity he didn't want to pass up, and then he casually added, "Maybe the governor will appoint *you*."

There's no way in the world she'll appoint me, I thought as I hung up the phone. I had never dreamed I would run for a seat in the House, much less the Senate. But Jim had planted a seed.

I cracked open the door and called my longtime friend and chief of staff, Joe McKeown, into my office to give him the news—though he would have heard soon enough on his own. In our age of social media, the whole world knew within thirty minutes. Joe and I headed to the airport an hour later, and I was caught up in a flurry of phone calls and texts. By the time I landed in Charleston, Senator DeMint's resignation dominated the news cycle. It was literally the talk of the town.

Every member of our delegation was certainly qualified to be our next senator, each with a unique skill set that would have served the state well. But even though the rare prospect of a Senate vacancy could easily have pitted one member against another, I never saw any of my colleagues try to position themselves at someone else's expense. As a Christian, I have learned to balance my personal ambition against the things I cannot control, and to trust in God's wisdom to guide my life. After several days passed and I had not heard anything from the governor's office, I assumed Governor Haley would appoint someone else, and I was at peace with that.

TREY

Some of our colleagues in the House look in the mirror and see a future governor, a potential US senator, or even a future president of the United States. Some of us look in the mirror and see ourselves in our backyards at home, playing catch with our dogs or pushing our children on a swing set. We see home, family, and a different, quieter life. Some of us want to serve for a season and then leave politics altogether. As I thought seriously about the opportunity, I realized that my ambitions did not extend to the US Senate. I decided it was better for South Carolina—and better for myself, frankly—if I chose to support one of the other candidates.

I was lucky to serve with a number of colleagues in the South Carolina delegation who would make excellent senators, but I knew if I tried to support everyone, I would actually support no one. As I talked with Mick, Jeff, and Tim, and with Joe Wilson, our state's veteran Republican representative, it seemed to make sense for all of us to get behind a consensus candidate—but I knew we had to move fast. The political jockeying was picking up steam as names began to surface and circulate. The decision belonged solely to Governor Haley, but it would make her decision easier if she didn't have five members of the US House competing for her attention. Perhaps that would inure to the benefit of one of us.

Tim Scott's name emerged immediately, of course. There was also mention of David Wilkins, former Speaker of the South Carolina House and US ambassador to Canada; Jenny Sanford, the former First Lady of South Carolina; Catherine Templeton, who headed the South Carolina Department of Health and Environmental Control; Henry McMaster, a former state attorney general (now the governor of South Carolina); and Mick Mulvaney.

As Governor Haley considered her options, she had a decision to make right up front: Would she pick a placeholder and create a level playing field for 2014, when the seat would be up for election and essentially open? Or would she pick someone who would commit to run for reelection, someone who had the name recognition and prowess to keep the seat? Wisely, she opted for the latter.

Mick was interested right from the start, but Tim wasn't sure whether he was interested or not. I had already decided I wasn't interested, and I did everything I could to take myself out of the running by saying nice things about the others—the ones I *knew* wanted the job. I am much more comfortable advocating for other people than I am advocating for myself. It wasn't difficult to say nice things about Tim Scott and Mick Mulvaney, but there was also a hint of selfishness in my advocacy for them. I was overwhelmed by the prospect of running my own statewide campaign.

If I were appointed and then ran for reelection, I knew the fund-raising would be nonstop, and I knew the arrows and daggers would come fast and furious, as they seemingly always do in political races—even intraparty races. That's the nature of the game if you're running for the Senate. There would be a contested and likely acrimonious primary in 2014 when Governor Haley's choice would have to defend the seat against challengers. I had already run against incumbent Republican officeholders in two primaries in my district, and I knew what a lonely and miserable experience it could be. I didn't want to revisit those emotions by running statewide against others who wanted the job more than I did, and I didn't want to have to raise the millions of dollars it would take to be competitive.

Those were some of the selfish reasons why I hoped Governor Haley would pick someone else, but there were also some practical reasons why I preferred Tim or Mick. Both would be better at the job than I would. Both are excellent at policy development. Both would be good fund-raisers. In my mind, both would make fantastic senators, but Governor Haley had earned the right to make the decision she thought was best. She had emerged to victory from a crowded GOP gubernatorial field, even when others had not given her much of a chance. Nikki Haley had not become governor without being smart, strategic, and able to assess political opportunities and realities with tremendous acumen.

Over the course of time, a list of three names began to emerge in the public domain: Tim Scott, Jenny Sanford, and Trey Gowdy. I don't know if these were really the top names that Governor Haley was considering—believe it or not, the media do not always get it right—but these three were discussed more than others, and they began to appear in multiple media accounts. I was ecstatic not only for Tim but also for the state of South Carolina. Tim would be the ideal choice on every level.

When I heard my name as part of the discussion, my initial thought was *What do I do now? It would seem self-serving and presumptuous for me to call the governor and ask her to remove my name from consideration. Maybe I'm not even on her list, and I would feel like an idiot if I asked her not to consider me when she wasn't considering me in the first place. Besides, who is dumb enough to remove himself from consideration for a seat in the US Senate?*

Surely I have many weaknesses and shortcomings, but I try to compensate for those with one solid strength: self-awareness. I recalled once again the advice I had received from Paul Ryan when I first entered the House in 2011: "Find what you're good at, and do that. Don't do the rest." Whether you call it self-awareness, discernment, or wisdom, it's necessary in life. I was convinced I could not effectively do the job or successfully run for reelection. I was not even planning to stay in politics past a certain point, so I hardly wanted a promotion. It sounds unambitious and weak, but it wasn't. I knew that Tim Scott would be exponentially better as a US senator than I would. He would be better for the state, better for the country, and a better selection for Governor Haley.

Governor Haley's chief of staff was a fellow former prosecutor and a friend with whom I could be forthright and brutally honest. I remember him asking me during a phone call, "If you are picked, Trey, would you commit to run for reelection?"

"I would have to, wouldn't I?" I said. "But you really should not pick me. I'm not being modest. I am not feigning humility. The best pick for Governor Haley, for the state, and frankly for me, is Tim Scott."

Publicly and privately, I let it be known: Tim Scott would be the best choice for South Carolina and for our country.

TIM

Advocating against yourself is rare in politics. Advocating *not* to be picked for the US Senate may be the rarest stance of all. It's one thing to be nice to each other in a private phone conversation, but it's another thing to openly and publicly endorse the other person. But that's what we did. I knew Trey would make an excellent senator.

As rumors continued to circulate, we talked on the phone several times a day. The conversation was similar every time, with each of us deferring to the other.

"What are you hearing?" I asked Trey.

"Nothing, except what they're reporting."

"Have you talked to the governor?"

"No, have you?"

"No. Do you want the job?"

"I'm not sure," he said. "I wish you would take it."

Before long, the media became interested in our individual and collective responses to the nomination. On December 13, 2012, the *New York Times* printed an article by Jennifer Steinhauer with the headline "Hoping for a Senate Seat, the Friendliest of Rivals." Her article read, in part,

> Representatives Trey Gowdy and Tim Scott, first-term Republicans from South Carolina, are both in the running to replace Senator Jim DeMint when the conservative leaves office next month. But they say they know the best man for the job: the other guy. . . .
>
> The competition for the opportunity to join the Senate without facing the voters—and gain an advantage for the next election—often inspires

backbiting and chilly discord among the hopefuls. But Mr. Scott and Mr. Gowdy are eating [together], praying [together] and heaping praise on each other through an experience that will absolutely end in great disappointment for one—if not both—in their search for ascent.

The two men cannot stop bantering—citing Bible verses, planning lunch, talking about legislation, the wisdom of law school versus no law school (Mr. Gowdy is a former prosecutor, Mr. Scott sold insurance) and debating which of them is more awesome.[1]

Meanwhile, it seemed that Governor Haley was talking to anyone and everyone who might like to be a senator—everyone, that is, except Trey and me. Neither one of us had received a call.

TREY

When the time came for her decision, Governor Haley made exactly the right choice—and Tim Scott's time in the US Senate has borne that out. Life works out like that sometimes. Tim is where he needs to be. Mick heads the Office of Management and Budget under President Trump, doing a job he is extremely well suited to do. And I am one step closer to the backyard of my home in South Carolina.

After his appointment in 2012, Tim worked incredibly hard over the next two years and won the right to finish out Senator DeMint's unexpired term. Then he worked just as hard from 2014 to 2016 to earn his own six-year term. One of the great honors of my life was to be with him on both election nights, in November 2014 and 2016, standing next to the first person of color to represent South Carolina in the US Senate since Reconstruction. My friend, who once represented the very swath of land where the Civil War began, now represents the entire state of South Carolina.

I remember the emotion Tim experienced when the 2014 race was called for him. I remember it so vividly because he was standing right beside me—in the city where I was born and that I now represent in Congress. The race was called at 7:06 p.m.—six minutes after the polls had closed, and well before any of the ballots had been counted. We embraced, and I whispered to him, "What took so long? This race should have been called six minutes ago." Tim's victory will forever be one of the highlights of my political life because it happened to someone whose political fortunes are every bit as important to me as my own.

The fact that Tim received word of his election to the US Senate in the Upstate region of South Carolina should tell you a lot about him. He chose to spend the evening of his historic election in *my* congressional district, with my wife, my children, and me.

If you know anything about South Carolina, you might wonder why a politician from Charleston—in the

Lowcountry—was in Upstate Greenville on election night. Why not Columbia, in the center of the state? Why not take the news in Charleston, where it all started for him? Without ever saying a word about it, it was Tim's way of honoring our friendship. When one friend succeeds beyond another, it can put pressure on the relationship. But true friends are there for each other, supporting each other, wanting the best for each other. Tim knew I was squarely in his corner, enjoying his epic victory right along with him. With his actions, he made it clear to everyone that he and I are in this together, that our friendship would only grow stronger. He was elected to the Senate, but nothing else had changed.

Tim does all the hard work of being a senator, and he shares all the good parts with me. For example, when Neil Gorsuch was nominated to the Supreme Court, Tim invited me to his office to meet him because he knew I loved the law. When a vote in the House delayed my arrival, Tim tried to keep Mr. Gorsuch in his office until I was free. (Who does that? Who stalls a soon-to-be Supreme Court justice so that his friend can run over to meet him?) Tim takes me onto the Senate floor every chance he gets. He offers to get me seating at Senate hearings that he knows will interest me. He includes me in meetings even when many other members of the House might not be included by their own senators. I may be the only member of the US House who doesn't aspire to the US Senate, and yet I get to live the job vicariously by watching my best friend in all of politics make his way in and through the upper house of Congress.

Rather than allowing ambition, pride, or self-interest to detract from our friendship, Tim and I have only grown closer since his promotion to the Senate. The entire appointment process, along with Tim's two subsequent campaigns, allowed me to see the quality of his character up close and personal. Through it all, our nascent friendship became an ironclad partnership tested by the fires of opportunity and success. For us, it is a partnership rooted in honesty, mutual respect, and fair dealing. It is rare, but possible, to be just as happy when something good happens to someone you care about as you would be if that something had happened to you.

TIM

Without a doubt, Trey Gowdy would have made an excellent US senator. Our country needs more leaders like him—people who are willing to set aside their own ambitions to do what they believe is best for someone else or for the nation. Trey would never say that he gave up his own shot at the nomination for me, but I can't think of another elected official who, if presented with the same opportunity, would have said, "Me? Hmmm, no thanks." Not for anybody. But that's what Trey did.

Now that I'm in the Senate, Trey and I have had to work a little harder to keep up some of the habits we developed when we were together in the House. For example, every year for the president's State of the Union address, Trey and I like to sit together. We've established this tradition because it makes the time more enjoyable and because we want to make sure we're singing from the same hymnbook, so to speak. When we're asked afterward how it went, I don't want to say, "That was the best speech I've ever heard!" while Trey is saying, "How'd that guy ever get elected?" We prefer to stay on the same page. Also, Trey needs help knowing when to stand and applaud.

When we were both in the House, we always sat together, but it's different now because all the senators sit together as a group. It has taken some maneuvering on Trey's part to preserve our tradition. People often ask us, "How do you guys always pull that off?"

The State of the Union address, like other joint sessions of Congress, is held in the House of Representatives, whose chambers are larger than the Senate's. House members have access throughout the day, and they can choose any seat they want in the main gallery, but they must remain in their chosen section and they cannot save seats for others. Senators have to walk from one side of the Capitol to the other to enter the House chambers at the appointed time, so we have a section set aside for us at the front.

Many have often joked that Congress is a lot like high school, with crowds, cliques, and special seating for seniors. In this case, the seniors are the senators. Trey and other friends in Congress joke that we are too old to walk fast enough to save our own seats.

Obviously, there is tremendous security all around the

Capitol complex for the State of the Union, but there is also extensive security on the floor of the House itself, with plenty of security guards and Capitol Police officers on hand to make sure the rules are enforced. Still, somehow or other, every single year, Trey manages to convince them to let us sit together. At an event that allows no saving of seats, Trey always saves me a seat. Not only that, but he somehow manages, as a member of the House of Representatives, to secure a seat in the section reserved for the Senate. I've never actually seen how he does it.

I'm always sensitive to the fact that he's holding a seat for me. I know that many other people would like to do what he's doing, so I try to get there as quickly as possible. As the senators are gathering, I work my way to the front of the line. But while Trey is waiting for me, there are usually some other guys from the House who also want to sit in the Senate's seats. I've seen officials become visibly unhappy with people trying to slip into that section, but they never seem to mind when Trey asks. With his experience as a prosecutor, I'm sure he can be pretty persuasive. Somehow, with his charm, he's able to finesse his way into those reserved seats.

TREY

Here's the truth of the matter. The Capitol Police and security teams deserve to be respected—they make it possible for us to be about the business of governing without having to fear

43

for our safety—and I always approach the security detail with respect. There's nothing wrong with being nice. Police officers appreciate kind words and respect as much as everyone else, and they probably deserve at least as much kindness and respect, if not more. I simply tell the officers the truth—that Senator Scott and I have been sitting together at the State of the Union for eight years now—and I let them decide.

It's not a test of power. The Capitol Police and security officers are in charge, and they have a duty. If the officer says no, then I'm done asking. I always say, "If you tell me no, I will understand completely and that will be the end of it. But can I sit on the very end until my friend Senator Scott arrives? If you run out of seats, you won't even have to ask me to leave. I'll excuse myself and we'll try again next year." I ask each time, and so far, the police and security guards have always said yes.

I'm very careful to defer to whatever they say. I also think they are kind to Tim and me because we are kind to them—not just on the night of the State of the Union, but on the other 364 days of the year as well. I never pass a police or security officer in the Capitol without speaking to him or her, and I always have my ID out, because I assume they will stop me. I don't wear the congressional lapel pin, so the police are not only free to stop me, they *should* stop me. I never assume they know who I am.

Every day, I wait to be searched and scanned like everyone else until they wave me through. Every day, I'm careful to make eye contact with the officers, and I wait for the okay to walk into restricted areas, because if I were a police officer, I would want members of Congress to be cognizant of all the moving parts the officers deal with every day. Of course, being a former prosecutor helps, because I know how tough the job of law enforcement is. I ask respectfully if I can sit with my friend who happens to be in the US Senate. I try to make it easy for them to say yes, all the while acknowledging that they can say no. It costs nothing to be nice and respectful, and in turn, the officers and security officials graciously allow two good friends to sit together during the State of the Union.

TIM

If they ever told Trey he couldn't sit with the senators, I would gladly give up my seat and move to the House section. There are some practical reasons why we sit together—we represent many of the same people, and we have similar political perspectives. But the main reason is that it's more meaningful and fun to experience history in the making when you have a friend to share it with.

Unusual friendships are born of many differences: class, religion, background, education, or any number of other things. Trey and I started with a lot in common, as two introverted South Carolinians with a passion for justice, shared political views, a spiritual prism to inform our conduct, and a love for both the Cowboys and the Gamecocks. Unlikely friendships are easy when things are going well. But eventually you will be tested by some sort of conflict that strikes the fault line of your differences—the part of your friendship that makes it unlikely. That's when you'll discover the true, underlying strength of your bond. You will quickly learn whether your friendship will survive, and perhaps even thrive, as you work through these circumstances. In many ways, our backgrounds and experiences were as different as black and white. And our connection was about to be tested.

3

"There's Been a Shooting in Charleston"

A Killer, a Race War, and a Senator's Best Friend

TIM

When I received the call about the shootings at Mother Emanuel, it hit me right in the heart. For a moment, I couldn't breathe, I couldn't think—I simply couldn't believe it. I've lived my entire life in Charleston, and my uncle Joe was a member of Mother Emanuel Church for fifty years. I know that historic church well. Furthermore, Clementa Pinckney was more than just my uncle's pastor. He was also a good friend of mine. We had served together in the South Carolina General Assembly; he was a state senator when I was in the House. Clementa was a giant among men, with a booming voice that sounded like heaven. But for all his passion and his commanding presence, he was gracious and unassuming. He didn't have to be the center of attention. Clementa was optimistic, smart, dedicated, clear thinking, and bipartisan. He didn't see the world as *us* versus *them*. He saw a world full of people to serve.

My first response was to take out my phone and call Clementa—but he didn't answer. So I sent him a text.

> I hear there was a shooting at the church tonight. Are you and your parishioners okay?

I waited for his reply. But my phone sat silent in my hand. I scrolled up to an earlier dialogue and read the one where he had texted me for tickets to President Obama's second inauguration. I was his go-to for stuff like that.

> I hope all is well. It's getting close to the big date. Where are my tickets?

I smiled when I read the one he sent just a few days after I had been appointed the new senator of South Carolina.

> Congratulations Senator. I am so happy and excited for you. You will be in my prayers as you serve us in Washington, Upper Chambers.

Clementa was one of the first to call me *Senator*. I remembered that day, that conversation, and our plans to work together on issues near and dear to both our hearts. Poverty. Education. Helping the community. We had so many ideas for the ways we would serve South Carolina to improve the lives of the people. We knew if we could show people that we were crossing party lines to work together, as a Democrat and a Republican, the community would be willing to work together too. The country had increasingly divided along partisan lines, and we knew we had to start somewhere. We had big plans.

I scrolled down again as I waited for Clementa's reply, but my phone was silent. No buzz to signal an incoming text.

With only limited information available anywhere, I reached out to my state staff in Charleston, to the sheriff's office, to every resource I could. I had a lump in my throat. I could not believe what was happening at a church in my hometown. When something as awful and paralyzing as this happens, you turn to your friends. I called Trey because I knew he would be there with me; and I knew that as a former prosecutor, he could understand the gravity of this horrific incident in ways that nobody else could.

I was scheduled to travel to an event on the West Coast the following morning, and of course I canceled that trip and planned my flight to Charleston. I was still in search of information when I received the call from sheriff's deputy Mitch Lucas with a message that would shatter my heart.

"Senator, I'm sorry to have to tell you that Clementa Pinckney was killed. He's gone."

I remember sitting in bed, stunned. *Oh, my God*, I prayed. *How is this possible, Father? How in the world is this possible?*

49

TREY

After Tim called me with the news about Mother Emanuel, I went online in search of information, but details were still scarce. I was reluctant to contact my friends in South Carolina state and federal law enforcement in the middle of an uncertain situation. If the shooter was still at large, the last thing they needed was a bunch of phone calls. But as the details of this unspeakable crime came to light throughout the evening and into the early morning hours, it became clear that this was a crime that would shock the citizens of our state, as well as the collective conscience of our nation.

Nine beautiful human beings were murdered at church. Nine fellow Christians. Nine fellow South Carolinians. Nine brothers and sisters, mothers and fathers, sons and daughters. They had studied the Bible with their killer. They had prayed with, and for, the man who would kill them. But they weren't murdered because they were Christians. They were murdered because they were black. The assailant wanted to start a race war. Claiming to be motivated by black-on-white crime, he premeditated and planned the mass killing of black Christians. It was a tragic convergence of hate, ignorance, malice, depravity, and evil.

Tim and I are native South Carolinians. Our love for our state began long before our public service and will endure long after our days in Washington are complete. We both acknowledge that South Carolina has a provocative history when it comes to matters of race. But the South Carolina of the past is different from the South Carolina where we want to grow old. Or at least we want it to be different. So this premeditated racial attack hit very close to home.

In the face of a crisis, Tim's first instinct is to run toward the solace of his faith. He turns to prayer and Scripture. I run to the facts, the evidence, and the justice system. But on this day, with our hearts broken for those whose lives were taken and for their loved ones, Tim and I also turned to the strength of our friendship for support. We found ourselves on a joint pursuit of meaning and understanding, in a battle against hopelessness. This act of barbarism had the potential to resurrect the pain of the past in a state that is so close to turning the corner toward the future. People of good conscience in South Carolina have spent decades writing a new chapter for our state, and suddenly a lone gunman had attempted to hijack the story line and send us spiraling back to the past.

When Tim and I talked the next morning, we came at the situation from different perspectives. Tim's response was both spiritual and emotional. His heart was telling him to catch the first flight home to Charleston, to be with the people in his community during this time of unspeakable pain. My instincts, as a former prosecutor and district attorney, were more procedural and pragmatic. *What can I do to help? What resources need to be made available? How solid is the evidence? Are there any surviving witnesses? Will the shooter be taken alive, commit suicide, or be taken down by law enforcement?*

I knew there was nothing I could do to aid in the investigation. The police in Charleston needed to process the crime scene, talk to the families of the victims, and search for a killer. Time was of the essence, and they had to focus on their work with as few distractions as possible. Former prosecutors—even a well-intentioned one—should stay completely out of the way and let the law enforcement professionals, forensic profilers, and crime scene specialists do their jobs.

As a member of Congress, I thought about the appearance of Tim's response. Would people understand if he went home and missed votes in the Senate? Would he be seen as a grieving member of the community or as a politician wanting to make the most of the situation? I know it sounds cynical, but politics is an unusual line of work. We're so often criticized for what we do and don't do that it becomes second nature to doubt our instincts. But Tim wasn't thinking about any of that. His heart was broken for his friends and for his community. Of course he went home. His heart was already there. He boarded the first plane the next morning.

In Washington, on the day after the shootings, there was a massive prayer vigil on the Capitol grounds. People of every background and political persuasion gathered to pray. It was beautiful and compelling to see the emotional boundaries lifted, to see people come together to comfort one another. It reminded me of all that is *good* about America. But why does it take a tragedy for us to come together so beautifully? Why must we face a calamity before we will join hands, pray, and seek healing?

TIM

I've always been impressed by what I call the "aftermath mentality." As Americans, we are so good at treating each other as individuals and family *after* a crisis. Think about 9/11. Think about hurricanes and other natural disasters. It is amazing to see how people will pull together to help, across all barriers and boundaries, when something bad happens. But I would like to see us develop an aftermath mentality *without* the crisis. Maybe we can avoid a future tragedy if we will act like the American family we are without waiting for an *event* to ignite that response.

Sadly, we all seem willing to go out of our way to avoid getting involved in everyday situations—like the priest and the Levite in the story of the Good Samaritan. They crossed to the other side of the road to avoid the man who had been beaten by robbers.[2] But if we will see the other person as an individual, as our neighbor, as part of *us*—regardless of our differences—perhaps we will become more willing to get involved, to help those who are hurting or who need a hand.

One example of this: A friend of mine who is a police officer started meeting with neighborhood kids who are growing up in single-parent homes. He has intentionally welcomed dozens of kids into his family by investing quality time to *avoid* a crisis.

Another example: My chief of staff, Jennifer DeCasper, is a busy single mother with very little discretionary time, yet she mentors young women who need direction in a city famous for its aggressiveness and individuality. Jennifer goes the extra mile because she believes in being the difference she wants to see.

I am proud of who we are after a crisis—as Americans, as Christians, as neighbors. I believe we can be like that *before* the crisis as well.

TREY

After the prayer vigil, I flew home to Upstate South Carolina. As soon as I landed, I called Tim.

"What can I do to help?" I asked. I could only imagine the calls he was fielding, the pulls he felt from his constituents and other officials. "Tell me the truth, Tim. Would it help you if I came to Charleston now, or should I wait and come down for the funeral?"

"Come later," he said. "If that changes, I'll let you know."

Though it was difficult not to be directly involved, I followed the advice of my friend and colleague and stayed upstate while Tim was in Charleston. Even from a distance, I was struck by how this tragedy had drawn everyone together. The crimes committed in Charleston were crimes against all South Carolinians and all people of good conscience. Everyone who was affected was drawn together in the bond of unity that often follows a crime that shocks the broader society.

People of every background, race, culture, and religion

gathered for vigils in Greenville and Spartanburg. The Upstate vigils were emotional, raw, and tragically beautiful as many people of color expressed forgiveness for the killer. I was struck by a profound realization: The assailant had aimed to start a race war, but he'd failed. Quite the opposite from what he intended, the aftermath of these killings offered lessons in forgiveness and reconciliation, led by the example of the victims' families, who spoke a clear and powerful message: "Love is always stronger than hate."[3]

TIM

If you know anything about the historic city of Charleston, it isn't difficult to imagine why Dylann Roof chose the Emanuel African Methodist Episcopal Church as his target. Known as Mother Emanuel because it birthed other AME churches, the church has endured more than its share of tragedies since its founding in 1816. Back then, all churches in Charleston were required to have a majority white membership, and blacks were allowed to meet for church services only during the day. African Americans were routinely harassed and forbidden to learn to read. Denmark Vesey, one of the church's founders, was implicated in a slave revolt and was later executed after a secret trial.

Six years after the church's founding, the original church building was burned to the ground by whites who were angry about black progress. The black congregation continued to meet in secret until the end of the Civil War, and then they rebuilt Mother Emanuel. In 1969, Coretta Scott King led a march from Mother Emanuel during the infamous hospital workers' strike. Throughout the church's history, great speakers such as Booker T. Washington, Dr. Martin Luther King Jr., and the Reverend Wyatt Tee Walker of the Southern Christian Leadership Conference often chose to speak at Mother Emanuel because of its historic importance. Mother Emanuel is a place of significance, history, and influence.

Perhaps a tougher question to answer is this: What led a young man to believe that starting a race war was possible in 2015, fifty years after the passage of the Civil Rights Act? The question is difficult, not because we don't know the answer, but because of what the answer says about where we stand as a nation.

Dylann Roof saw the cracks in the foundation of our society, where people have begun to retreat into their own echo chambers, removing themselves from the melting pot into individual bowls based on "identity." Republicans, you watch these channels and read these news outlets over here. Democrats, your channels and news outlets are on the opposite side of the dial. The tragic deaths of more than a few black men, from Trayvon Martin to Michael Brown to Walter Scott, have inflamed racial tensions to levels not seen in decades. We have divided ourselves by religion, race, and relativity, with statements such as "That may be *your* truth, but it's not *my* truth." We are divided by gender and geography, by ideology, identity, and every idiosyncrasy we can imagine. Research even shows that conservatives are relocating to live where other conservatives live, and liberals are moving to liberal cities.[4] We are decoupling our nation's amazing diversity.

And yet, through the tragedy at Emanuel, there came a glimpse of the future we must choose. The families of the Emanuel Nine could have shown the world their anger; they could have given Dylann Roof exactly what he wanted. However, their faith and righteousness showed us all another path. They called for peace and unity. On national television, they forgave the man who killed their mothers, fathers, brothers, and sisters. Because of them, Charleston came together in a way not seen before in my lifetime. The eyes of the nation turned to South Carolina, expecting more violence and death, and instead they saw a celebration of life and the power of faith.

We must see to it that the Emanuel Nine did not die in vain. We are the American family, first and foremost, and that is a bond that we cannot allow to be broken. We must find ways to overcome the sensationalism, the anger, and the divisiveness that have cast a shadow over our nation.

Clementa Pinckney and I planned to work across partisan lines for the betterment of all. I won't allow those plans to evaporate just because he's gone. And I won't accept racial discord as a fact of life. I want to honor Clementa and the eight other precious souls who went to join the Lord that Wednesday night.

On the Sunday after the shootings at Emanuel, I told my wife, Terri, that I felt like attending an African American church, but I couldn't explain why. When I woke up that morning, I felt a sense of hopelessness. It was a familiar feeling. I felt the same anger I had known as a prosecutor, when my faith was so often rattled by crimes against innocents.

How could a loving God allow that to happen?

How could God allow women and men to be slaughtered in his house while reading his Word and sharing his love with a stranger, as he had commanded them to do? These challenges to my faith had driven me out of the criminal justice system in the first place, and the cynicism that arose pervaded all facets of my life, including my spiritual beliefs. By the end of my sixteen years as a prosecutor, my mother and my wife had both seen me grow disdainful toward "religious answers," and they agreed that a decade and a half of seeing depravity on a daily basis was enough for me.

Now I felt those emotions coming back. I wanted to go to a church with people of color because I needed to be with folks who would share and reflect my anger. I wanted to be with people who would shake their fists in the face of God and, like the prophet Habakkuk, ask how a merciful, loving God could possibly allow wicked to prevail over good.

I chose to attend a service at Cornerstone Baptist Church, pastored by my longtime friend the Reverend Charles J. J. Jackson. Pastor Jackson had been a source of comfort and guidance when I was a prosecutor. I liked him. I respected him. I hoped he would capture the anger and cynicism of what had happened in Charleston. So I drove to his church, fully expecting to step into a congregation of people who were angry along with me.

I could not have been more wrong.

I parked in the church parking lot and walked toward the entrance with my head down. When I entered the church vestibule, a young black couple greeted me and politely asked if I was visiting. When I said yes, they welcomed me and invited me to sit with them. Though my intention was to remain as inconspicuous as I could, I think I assumed they probably knew who I was. I had grown up in Spartanburg and now lived only a few miles away. I had been a district attorney in town, my father was a doctor there, my wife is well known in the community, and I was currently their congressman. I had even visited the church before, and I had friends who attended regularly. Surely they knew who I was, and I presumed that's why they felt comfortable befriending me.

As we sat down in our pew, some friends from Cornerstone began to stop by to say hello. First an older black man, and then a younger couple. Each one shook my hand and thanked me for visiting. After the third person stopped by our pew to speak to me, a pattern became evident. The woman who had first invited me to sit with her family turned to me, smiled, and asked, "Excuse me, but who are you? People seem to know you."

At that moment, a stunning awareness hit me: This couple who had invited me to sit with them during the church service had no idea who I was. When I walked into the building that morning, I was a white stranger entering their black church community just four days after a white stranger had murdered nine black people at a church. Still, they had welcomed me without hesitation. How could they be so warm and trusting with a white visitor so soon after that unspeakable tragedy? Hadn't they learned from the vulnerability of the church members in Charleston? Surely they would be on guard for any new faces, wouldn't they? Surely they would be suspicious of a random white visitor. Surely they would not have been so hospitable unless they knew me. Right?

Tears began rolling down my face as the service began, and I experienced the broadest spectrum of emotions. I felt humbled by their grace and trust. I felt enraged because innocent people who dared to welcome a stranger had been killed. I felt anger that God had let these people die while they studied the Bible. Most of all, I felt ashamed that I was angry in the presence of such humility, trust, and grace. The real victims—black Christians—were the ones opening their arms, welcoming a stranger into their circle, and inviting him to worship alongside them.

Cornerstone Baptist Church was exactly the wrong place for me to go to wallow in anger and question God. Instead, Reverend Jackson preached a beautiful sermon on forgiveness, faith, and trusting God.

I did not want to hear any of it. I needed to hear all of it.

The following Friday, I drove to Charleston for Clementa Pinckney's funeral. Tim and I had agreed to meet downtown, but I wanted to make sure he was okay, so I made an excuse to go by his house. When I arrived, I saw that Senator James Lankford of Oklahoma, a former House colleague, had also stopped by to see Tim. James is one of the most authentic and committed Christians I know in public service. He is a genuinely good and thoughtful person, and I was grateful that he had come to lift Tim's spirits.

After we drove together into Charleston, we gathered with others on a bus and rode to the site of the funeral. When Tim and I walked in, virtually every person stopped him for a conversation. I cannot pretend to know what it's like to be a conservative black Republican and to be viewed with skepticism by people on all sides. Because I know Tim so well, I know he feels the tension, but he is always gracious toward everyone.

In the days between the murders at Emanuel and the memorial service at the College of Charleston, Tim attended several vigils and memorials. At some of those gatherings, even though he was the highest-ranking elected official in attendance, even though he lives in Charleston, and even though he had a family connection within Emanuel, he was not asked to speak. Why? Because he's a Republican? Even when some of the barriers had come down, others remained. But rather than make a point of it, Tim ignored the slights, focusing instead on the legacy of those who were slain and the remarkable response of their families.

Most people will never see the slights Tim endures for being black and conservative. Most will never know the dark nights of the soul when he wonders whether he fits with either group. Most will never see the ache and frustration because he hides it so well behind a beautiful smile. This comes from decades of personal experience where he has had to hide it.

Inside the auditorium at the College of Charleston, Tim and I were ushered into a room to wait for the memorial service to begin. It was just the two of us there until Congresswoman Tulsi Gabbard and her husband, Abraham, joined us. At first glance, it might seem unusual for a progressive Democratic congresswoman from Hawaii, who happens to be Hindu, to offer support and comfort to a black evangelical Christian who also happens to be a Republican senator from South Carolina. But for those of us who are fortunate to know Tulsi Gabbard, it was not unusual at all. She was precisely the right person to offer comfort to Tim.

Tulsi is one of the finest people we know. She is thoughtful, compassionate, and kind. She has inner strength gained from serving our country with valor as a combat veteran, coupled with the outward beauty of someone who believes and lives the spirit of aloha. She listens. She is quiet when she senses that silence is best. Her silent strength is contagious.

Hawaii is a long way from South Carolina. With the funeral coming at the beginning of the Fourth of July break in Congress, Tulsi had every reason in the world to go home and offer prayers or good thoughts for the people of South

Carolina from her home state. But she didn't go home. She came to South Carolina to mourn, to pray, to love, and to be silent when the questions were too big for answers. I will be forever grateful to Tulsi and Abraham for coming to the funeral, caring for Tim, and being so supportive of South Carolina in the wake of such a tragedy.

Tulsi did something else I found remarkable. She was seated a few chairs away from me during the service, which included singing and dancing. Tulsi is not African American, she is not a Methodist, and she is not from South Carolina. But there she was, participating fully in the worship service. She sang. She danced. She honored the faith of those around her, even though it was not her own. That is a rare quality, but that is Tulsi, and that is why she is one of my favorite people in all of government. Tulsi crosses lines to connect with people on the other side. Of course, Tulsi doesn't vote the same way that Tim and I do in Congress. We represent different states and different districts with different constituents who have different political beliefs. But the differences in how we vote seem small in light of our similarities in the rest of life.

The service lasted several hours, punctuated with moments of inspiration. President Obama spoke and gave considerable focus to the forgiveness and Christian charity shown by the family members of those who had been killed. The president ended his remarks by singing "Amazing Grace," and it was a conciliatory moment that everyone could feel. Reconciliation is what we needed that day. We yearned for it.

After the service, after we said good-bye to our colleagues

from all parts of the United States, Tim hosted a meal for friends and family at a restaurant on the water. Charleston is such a beautiful city, where the past and the present collide in a naturally stunning setting, with the narrow roads, the marshes, and the historic buildings. The heartbeat of South Carolina is in Charleston, with her rich, provocative history and boundless potential. Some South Carolinians refer to Charleston as the Holy City because of the religious freedom found there hundreds of years ago. We're all aware of the low points in our history as well. Charleston is where South Carolina's whole story is on full display against a background as beautiful as any in the world.

As I wrestle with the aftermath of the Charleston tragedy coupled with where we are as a nation, I come back to the same important questions: Why does it take a calamity to lead us toward reconciliation? How long can reconciliation last when it is born of adversity? Why does it seem we're wired to show the most kindness and the greatest compassion in the days following violence or disaster? Can we not capture this energy, this goodwill, this sense of inclusion, on good days as well?

TIM

When I got that call on the night of the Emanuel Church shooting, my heart broke. But one of the blessings that arose from that tragedy was exactly the opposite of the killer's intention. My friendship with Trey grew stronger in the days and weeks that followed. It was a powerful moment for me when I realized that the Good Lord had prepared in advance the friendship I would need during this very challenging time. God, in his infinite wisdom, strategically placed Trey and me in the state where the power of uncommon bonds could be seen during a divisive time.

Even between people with no previous relationship, this racially motivated atrocity actually bridged a racial divide. Love is always stronger than hate, and God's love is stronger than anything. If we want to move forward, we must anchor ourselves in the powerful, transformative, and genuine love of God.

4

Like the Friends of Job

A Tough Assignment and
a Congressman's Best Friend

TREY

Toward the end of my second term in Congress, with my best friend from the House now over in the Senate, I began to notice that making the weekly trip to Washington was harder and harder. I didn't love being in politics in the first place, and I felt that even more so now. During my time in Washington, I'd had some bills signed into law, I had established a reputation for asking some good questions from time to time in committee, and I was on TV a fair amount. But accomplishing things is pretty difficult when you are one of 435 members of a legislative body. I thought I had done a good job of representing my district, but I found it difficult to gain a real sense of accomplishment in Congress.

I had no aspirations to the US Senate (I had already proven that), nor was I interested in running for governor of South Carolina or any other statewide office back home. I knew my constituents weren't thinking I would serve for just four years and then quit, but most days during that time I was ready to be done and go back to the legal system, where things just seem to make more sense to me.

Politics is very different from the criminal justice system—the end objective is different, the process is different, and there's no referee or judge to keep things fair. As a prosecutor, you always know who your client is: Lady Justice. She is always right, and she is never unreasonable. She doesn't have expectations that cannot reasonably be met. She simply asks for fairness and justice. In politics, the objective is to win. And as the political environment becomes increasingly relativistic, winning (or desiring to win) seems to justify or rationalize all else.

In the criminal justice system, evidence is thrown out if procedural errors are made in the collection of that evidence. Confessions are suppressed if there were violations in the manner they were sought or obtained. Some critics dismiss these as examples of "technicalities," but technical errors rarely result in suppressed evidence. The manner in which things are done *matters*, and "technical" errors are really unconstitutional errors—even with all good intentions among the police or the prosecutors.

In politics, the end seems to justify the means. It is seemingly okay to misrepresent facts about a political opponent, to take facts out of context, to steal yard signs and push telephone calls—to do anything you deem necessary to win. Winning is all that matters in modern-day politics. Actions are approved—or at least tolerated—so long as they are done on behalf of the "right" team.

The criminal justice system doesn't work that way. The end does not justify the means. The process matters every bit as much as the end result. I value fairness. To be described as "fair" by a critic is the highest compliment one can receive, and it is exceedingly rare in the modern political culture. I strive to always be fair, and I missed the fairness of the courtroom.

I remember the restaurant table where Tim and I were sitting when I told him I wanted to go home to resume the practice of law. He didn't reply with logic or persuasion. He went straight to the approach I hate the most. He played the friendship card.

"I would like you to stay for one more term," he said. "It would mean the world to me."

What Tim was saying, and what I knew to be true, was that Washington can be a very lonely town, and friendships are hard to come by. It was important to Tim that I stay because I was his best friend in politics; I'm someone he can trust to discuss anything and everything. So I understood why he was asking me to stay. I would have done the same thing if our roles had been reversed.

"Brother, I love you," I said. "But I do not love you that much. I can't do it."

He painted a picture for me of things left undone, opportunities to be seized, and then he appealed to our common faith, saying there was more that God still had for me to do in Washington.

I believe there are dozens of people, if not more, in Upstate South Carolina who could effectively represent the district in Congress. Every representative is replaceable. I certainly am. If we ever lose sight of the fact that there are others who can—and deserve a chance to—hold political office, we have already fallen victim to the greatest of all political sins: pride.

I really didn't want to consider it, but I told him I would discuss it one more time with my wife. She is a real-life angel with the sweetest and most selfless spirit of anyone I have ever known. Terri is not a political person at all. She rarely follows politics, as she is much more interested in what her first grade students are learning and doing. True to her nature, she told me she would be on board with whichever choice I made: to come home or run again.

When I called Tim back, he doubled down, coming over to the House from the Senate to give me all the reasons I should stay—and he persisted, telling me again how much it would mean to him if I would hang in for one more term.

"Just one more term, Trey," he said. "That's it. Next time, I won't even ask."

Finally, I agreed to run for reelection—because Tim Scott persuaded me to. I stayed. And I have not yet forgiven him for that.

A few months after those conversations with Tim,

I received a phone call that would change my DC experience in a dramatic way. Taking a quick break from cutting the backyard grass at home in Spartanburg, I went inside to check my phone and discovered a missed call from then–Speaker of the House John Boehner. When I called him back, he said, "Gowdy, I'm leaning toward a select committee to look into Benghazi, and I want you to be on it. I'll call you back later this afternoon. Don't say anything yet. It's still not final."

"Yes, sir, Mr. Speaker, I won't say anything until you tell me to," I said. Then I asked, "Mr. Speaker, do you think I have time to mow the front yard before you call me back?"

"Ha!" He laughed the laugh that all of us who worked with him had heard a thousand times. "Yes, Gowdy, you can go mow the front yard."

My mind was racing as I finished cutting the grass, and I'm sure I missed more than a few spots. I wondered what the Speaker had in mind in terms of panel members, how the committee would be constructed, and what its jurisdiction would be. When Speaker Boehner called back that afternoon, he had not only decided to convene a select committee, but he had decided that I would chair that committee. Life was going to get a lot more complicated.

When I later had permission to discuss it and I told Cindy Crick, my longtime chief of staff, her response was immediate and to the point: "Maybe Tim Scott was right. Maybe there is one more thing you need to do here in DC."

That "one more thing" proved to be the single most

difficult professional challenge I have ever had. Over the next two years—the two toughest years of my professional life—the same sardonic thought went through my head hundreds of times: *Don't blame God for this. Blame Tim Scott.*

People who follow politics, and especially those who followed the 2012 story of what happened in Benghazi, Libya, have already made up their mind about those events. My purpose in bringing it up here is certainly not to reopen that chapter. I have no desire to get sucked back into that sensitive and polarizing vortex. I am at peace with what the committee was asked to do, why the House asked us to do it, and the work we did. I understand there are critics, and they are certainly entitled to their opinions.

The facts are neither Republican nor Democratic, but those facts are important to the families of those who were killed, as well as the men who survived the attacks. Four Americans were killed: Ambassador J. Christopher Stevens, US Foreign Service Information Management Officer Sean Smith, and CIA contractors Tyrone S. Woods and Glen Doherty. Stevens was the first US ambassador killed in the line of duty since 1979. I do not know the political perspectives of any of the men involved. I only know that they were all what we strive to be: honorable, brave, willing to help others, and proud to serve our country. As fellow Americans—regardless of our political leanings—we can honor the sacrifice made by brave fellow citizens in a faraway land. As polarizing as the issues may have been, at least we can all agree that the four who died and those who survived are heroes.

My only reason for mentioning Benghazi is to highlight the immeasurable value of friendship when we face our most difficult challenges. Tim was of incalculable aid and comfort to me during that time. It was an incredibly lonely time—probably the loneliest extended season I can remember in my life. The hearings lasted two years, so there were a lot of really long days, and my time with Tim was a sanctuary that I could look forward to. You know the friendship is real when your friend is willing to stand with you through your darkest hours.

TIM

I remember those days well, and like Trey, I wouldn't want to go back. When he was charged with the responsibility of leading the Benghazi investigation, Trey approached the issue as a prosecutor in search of the truth—not as an elected official, not as a partisan. He didn't accept the chairmanship with a political motivation—which was quintessential Trey (he's actually not very partisan)—but the investigation quickly became politicized. That was never Trey's intention. His goal was to find and deliver the truth for the benefit of the families of those who died. History will judge how well he and the panel succeeded.

When I watched Trey walk into the Capitol Hill Club, night after night, with that weight on his shoulders, I saw his transparency and I sensed his vulnerability. It wasn't articulated, but it was tangible, and it proved to me his authenticity and sincerity. He had a sacrificial, passionate desire to bring resolution to the families. But what I saw in Trey that really took our friendship to a new level was the humility and determination with which he bore that burden.

As Trey has said, it was the most draining, negative, and difficult time in his life, even though he's a man who used to try murder cases for a living. The investigation required hundreds of hours of preparation along with hours of asking questions and hearing testimony. But because I understood the problems he was facing, I knew he did not need more questions or "advice" about the hearings. He needed to share the burden, not hash it out over dinner.

The best response, from my perspective, wasn't to try to help him dissect what was going on in the hearing room. I simply offered space to have normal conversations, and sometimes we shared a meal without *having* to talk at all. Sometimes in a friendship, we build credibility and trust not by what we *say*, but by what we're willing to *share*. A friend can help shoulder the burden without dissecting it. Sometimes the gift of presence is worth more than a thousand words.

TREY

What I loved most about Tim Scott during that season was this: If I asked him for advice, he gave it. His political acumen has always been much higher than mine; he understands strategy better than I do—*how* to do things, *why* to do things. I don't want to say he's a better politician, because that makes him sound inauthentic when there's not a disingenuous bone in his body. But he is better *at* politics than I am. And it's not because he sought to become politically savvy; he's just good at it.

With Benghazi, he could have advised me in dozens of ways, but I remember very clearly how little advice he offered. In fact, he never even brought up the topic of Benghazi. He never once said, "So, tell me what disastrous thing happened today." Instead, he guided me into conversations about the Cowboys—which I am always up for—and anything else we could talk about that had nothing to do with the hearings. He was like an optimistic, hope-filled oasis in an otherwise desolate professional time. (I'm assuming an oasis can be bald and built like a middle linebacker.)

Tim's approach reminded me of the biblical story of Job, who suffered calamities far worse than anything most of us will ever experience. I'm not in any way comparing myself to Job, but when he went through those difficulties in his life, the people who meant the most to him, the ones who comforted him the most, were those who came and sat with him and didn't say a word. Yes, those same people later broke their silence and went on for page after page, questioning Job and offering him advice, but they were most effective when they sat and remained silent. They were simply there for him.

Far greater than any piece of advice Tim could have offered was the sacred gift of his presence and his friendship, an hour and a half at the end of the day when nobody would tell me what I was doing wrong or give me suggestions on how to do this, that, or the other. To provide a sanctuary or a safe harbor to a friend in need is the greatest gift you can give.

I remember walking out of the meeting room after one particularly difficult day, and the first two faces I saw were Tim Scott's staffers. For a brief moment, because of the smiles on their faces, everything seemed just a little bit better. I was soon brought back to reality when I faced the media gaggle, where there were no smiles to greet me, but that brief interlude was enough to keep me going. Though Tim has never owned up to it, I remain convinced that he sent those two people, whose faces I would immediately recognize, to be there when I walked out. It was his way of saying, "We're with you, no matter what."

When things are going well in politics, you have a ton of friends. If things aren't going quite as well, there's an awkward silence. The thing I look for is this: Will this person still return my phone calls when I'm not a member of Congress? When I don't have any money? When I don't have any influence? When I'm just like everybody else, will I still matter to this person? The best test of someone's true loyalty is whether he or she is still willing to be your friend when you're going through a difficult time. There's a profound security in knowing that someone in your life will somehow love you even *more* as things get worse.

It may not amaze you to hear that Tim Scott, my fellow

Republican and South Carolinian, was a good and supportive friend during this challenging time in my life. But you might be surprised to know how much support and encouragement I received from Democrats in Congress—which some would consider the most unlikely of sources.

Sadly, in our current political culture, the idea that a Democrat would offer a Republican a private word of support, or vice versa, would not be lauded by all. But Tim and I are trying to move the debate from one of *conflict* to *contrast*, with a hopeful eye toward *conciliation*.

Contrast refers to those differences that arise naturally from our life experiences—we come from different areas and different backgrounds; we have different styles and different perspectives; we approach issues from different angles and see different solutions to problems.

Conflict speaks to those areas where we've dug in our heels on our differences. Those differences seem preeminent, and as we retreat to one camp or the other, life becomes defined by the contrast. Conflict is debilitating in a relationship. Still, despite the constant pressure in Washington to focus on our differences, I sense a hunger in our nation, at least among those not on the ballot, to focus on what we all have in common.

With that in mind, I can tell you there are plenty of Democratic colleagues who offer words of comfort during difficult times. And there are plenty of Republicans who do the same for Democratic colleagues going through personal angst or struggle. We may disagree on most policy initiatives, but when it comes to seeing someone through a dark chapter, faith and humanity are higher values than political expediency. I am grateful to everyone who is as willing to help on a personal level as they are to contend on a professional level.

TIM

The Benghazi process dragged on for more than two years. Imagine facing opposition—every minute and every hour of every day, for months on end. That kind of pressure can consume your life. The investigation took over everything on Trey's docket, and the expectations only became more intense. Find something new and the Democrats would attack; find nothing new and the Republicans would attack. It was painful to watch.

The truth is, if you're in politics and you're impervious to pain, you probably should get out. I never want to get to the point where the attacks don't hurt anymore. I want my nerve endings connected and functioning. It's a dangerous person who no longer feels the pain. It might be expedient in a political world that's all about process, but it's hazardous for a person's character.

Seeing Trey's resilience and integrity under fire only increased my respect for him as a colleague and a great friend. All his other responsibilities didn't cease just because he was chairing the Benghazi committee. I was flabbergasted at the load he was able to bear in a political environment that he so strongly disliked. Back when we were starting out in Washington together, I think he got some of the worst committee assignments. But he was faithful with what he was given, and his diligence and integrity were ultimately rewarded when he was elevated to the chairmanship of the Benghazi committee. I'm not sure he was all that excited about the honor, but it was no small thing. If he has more gray hair now than he did before, it's only because of the wisdom he gained—and the difficulty he endured—while stepping up to a tremendous responsibility in a very high-profile situation.

I'm a little more emotional than Trey is, and I like to talk about the issues that are important to me. Trey listens well, and he gives me the benefit of his wisdom and experience with sound advice. I count as a real privilege those times when I've been able to give back to him as someone who is willing to shoulder the load when he needs it.

I could sense the pressure he was under. I could see it. I could feel the weight on his shoulders, having to lead that effort. He was slowly being pushed into the ground. I wanted to shoulder the load with him—he's my brother. When your brother is sluggish under the weight of what he's carrying, you lean under the burden and carry it with him.

It didn't feel like an extraordinary decision. It didn't even feel heavy.

It felt like an honor.

How did I walk with him? I took off my shoes and put

my feet up, and I listened to him. I was his best friend in Washington, and I was happy for the chance to play that role.

Being there for each other is a cornerstone in any committed friendship. Imagine how much more powerful it could be across the nation if our presence, our support, and our desire to understand were applied at the very point of our differences.

5

What We Have in Common

Building a Friendship to Last

When I was running for the South Carolina House of Representatives in 2008, knocking on doors was a very important part of campaigning. This is a fantastic opportunity to meet constituents, and it's the best way I've ever found to gain a firsthand understanding of their interests and concerns.

One of my volunteers that year was a guy named Pete, a retired police officer from New York City who had recently moved to our county. He and his son, Tom, were both dedicated volunteers. One morning, to my great surprise, Pete showed up wearing a T-shirt with a Confederate flag on the front, and he was carrying a 9mm handgun. (It was concealed, but anyone could see the bulge.)

We were as unlikely a pairing as you could find—a black guy going door-to-door with a guy wearing a Confederate flag. I could only imagine the kind of looks we might get.

I didn't tell Pete to put on a different shirt, even though I knew it could be offensive to the people of color we met that day. Then again, my presence could be offensive to other folks we might meet.

This could easily become a lose-lose situation.

Nevertheless, we headed out together and spent the next three or four hours knocking on doors. Along the way, we talked about Pete's former work in law enforcement, my dreams for the district, and everything in between. Funny thing was, it turned out to be a great day, and we learned we had a lot in common.

At one house, we walked up to a couple of white guys who were working on a car. One of the men looked up, glanced at the rebel flag on Pete's shirt, and then looked at me. Then he did a double take: He looked at Pete again, and then looked back at me. After an awkward moment, he smiled and said, "Hey, man!"

Now that the ice had been broken, the four of us talked for a while, and I left the guys one of my campaign signs for their yard. They were actually some of the nicest people we met that day, though they were completely thrown off by the dichotomy that Pete and I represented. Making the rounds with Pete was one of the highlights of my campaign season. He became one of my best volunteers and a good friend.

On a different day, I was out again going door-to-door, but Pete wasn't with me. When my team and I approached a house with a Confederate flag waving on a pole in the front yard, I paused for a moment and thought, *Where's Pete when you need him?* My friend and his T-shirt would have given me a conversation starter and possibly some instant rapport. But this time I was on my own. The volunteers who were with me were reluctant to go into the yard. They thought I was crazy to knock on the door, and I probably was. But when you're seeking votes, you'll take chances you might not otherwise take. In some races, you have to knock on enough doors to win, and I couldn't afford to pass one up, Confederate flag or not.

When the gentleman who lived there answered the door, he looked a bit surprised, as I had anticipated. But it turned out he was conservative and wanted the same things I wanted. Ultimately, he didn't care if I was black, white, or polka-dotted, as long as I was conservative. Though there were many things that might have separated us, what drew us together were our common values. Before I left him that day, he had put a sign in his yard. Actually, I think he asked for two.

Our perception of people is too often colored by preconceived notions and expectations, whether those are based on past experience or shaped by cultural norms and attitudes. Ultimately, as a black politician in the Deep South, you can be certain that a good ol' boy in a rebel T-shirt is not going to vote for you. Unless you're wrong.

TREY

Tim gets exponentially more invitations to give keynote talks than I do, and his venues are always much bigger than mine. He also accepts a lot more of those invitations than I would. Still, I delight in the fact that I get to participate behind the scenes.

Every once in a while, he'll say at dinner, "Okay, can we talk this through? Here's what I'm thinking . . ." I love that I get to be an anonymous contributor to one of his speeches. If it goes well, I can know I gave him that funny line. If it doesn't go well, I can say, "Hmm? What? No, I had no idea that Tim Scott was speaking anywhere tonight." It works well for both of us.

I remember the night he told me he was going to deliver a "roast" at the Washington Press Club Foundation Dinner on March 1, 2017. Tim was to be the featured Republican speaker at this charity event of journalists and lawmakers at the Ritz-Carlton Hotel.

The Washington Press Club Foundation's mission is to fight for education, equality, and excellence in journalism. At their annual dinner, a selected member of Congress does a comedy routine. It's a very tough audience, and some members of Congress have bombed in epic fashion as they tried to be funny at this event. Tim has found himself in some contentious situations in politics, but this one seemed unnecessary to me.

I asked, "Who in the world told you this would be a good idea?"

I remember the look on Tim's face, and it was pure panic.

That's when I realized the plane had already left the ground. His staff had already accepted the invitation, and he had committed to do it. I thought he was asking me *if* he should do it, but he was actually asking me *how* he should do it. There is a big difference between *if* and *how.*

If there's anything I hate in life, it's when someone waits until after something has happened and then tells me what I should have done differently. That's not what Tim needed now. It was time to shift our focus. My job was not to tell him what a bad idea this was. My job was to help him get ready. Our only choice was to move forward and make this reality as good as it could be. The roast was going to happen, and most of Washington would be watching Tim's first foray into comedy. He needed to do well.

TIM

Trey definitely gave me a sense of urgency. I remember him saying, "Your timing and delivery will be of crucial importance. If you miss with your timing, they will miss your joke, and you will be the laughingstock of Washington."

What Trey said was exactly what I needed to hear. He showed me the difference between being sensitive and being honest. Trey was sensitive to my circumstances, and I needed for him to be honest in his evaluation of my jokes. The last thing either of us wanted was for me to go out there and flop, especially because stand-up comedy is not my strong suit.

I like to think of myself as a nice guy, and saying yes to requests is natural for me. Trey's reaction when he heard what I had committed to was straight to the point. If he had been more concerned about my feelings than about speaking the truth, if he had said, "Oh, you'll be fine, you've got this," I can tell you right now, that would *not* have been helpful. I needed a friend who would look me straight in the eye and say, "Seriously, dude, you are out of your element." I needed that kind of clarity. He gave me a definite sense of urgency, and I took the challenge seriously. By the end of the next evening, I had ten jokes. Most were pretty funny, but a few were too far outside the lines. We got busy reining them in.

If I had it to do over again, I would probably go to a movie instead of speaking at the Press Club dinner. Why in the world did I ever say yes? I am not by nature funny, and my personality is not the type that likes to roast people. The audience at the dinner is always a tough crowd, and I don't think my speech would have gone as well as it did without Trey's help. Reporters asked me afterward if Trey would be okay that I used his hair as a punch line. I told them, "He not only let me joke about his hair, he actually wrote one of the punch lines for me."

TREY

I was more nervous for Tim that night than I would have been if it had been me. I know how good his brand is, and I wanted to protect that for him. I also know that careers can be damaged at the Washington Press Club Foundation Dinner. One colleague who accepted a similar invitation to do a comedy routine at the dinner awoke the next morning to headlines like these: "Congressman Weirds Out Washington" and "Worst Speech Ever." So, initially, there was some cause for concern for Tim.

But he did what he always does: He prepared, and then he excelled. His speech was well received, and he was the single biggest congressional star for the rest of the week. I was thrilled for him. Honestly, I'm happier that he was successful than I would have been if I had delivered the speech myself. (That's chiefly because I never, ever would have accepted that invitation. I definitely don't have the guts to do what he did.)

The way I look at it is this: Because we're friends, what's good for Tim is good for me. When he succeeds, I succeed. We can build real trust with others by stepping into their story, by committing our time and attention to what matters to them. When we walk the path together with a trusted friend, when his or her success is as important to us as our own, then we're really on to something special.

As you seek to build rapport and trust with someone, you must be willing to see the world from a perspective that is not your own. If you will devote the effort and energy it takes to develop a connection with someone, I think you'll find you have a lot in common with most people.

The 24/7 news cycle we have today so often seems to focus on differences and divisions within our nation. But as I talk to people one-on-one, I find a universal hope and desire for unity. I earnestly believe most people of good conscience are tired of the constant fighting and the resulting feelings of disunity. You could put any two people of good conscience together, and regardless of whatever differences they might have, you would find that they agree on *most* things in life.

So why do we have such a tendency in our society to run toward what divides us? It's baffling to me. Yes, we have our differences, and we always will, but at this point in life, I am much more interested in focusing on what brings us together.

It's amazing how much you can learn from someone if you will simply engage in a conversation, be willing to listen, and seek to understand. Even though I've lived half a century in the South, I always find it shocking to see racial prejudice manifest itself. It would be exponentially worse to experience it firsthand. Though I have never personally experienced the humiliation that African Americans have felt from being fire-hosed during protest marches, being denied service at retail businesses, or having to look for separate facilities for basic human needs, there is value in trying to understand. When we ask people to tell their stories, we can better understand their framework for life.

Democratic South Carolina Congressman Jim Clyburn is both a colleague and a friend. Though he and I don't often vote the same way, our delegation sticks together well on matters affecting our beloved home state. Mr. Clyburn represents the part of South Carolina where my parents grew up, and we share a love for golf. Frankly, that's enough to get a conversation started.

The airports in Washington, DC, become very bipartisan on fly-out days. Democrats and Republicans alike are looking forward to getting home to be with their families. You get to know your fellow representatives in a different setting as you jointly hope the weather will remain clear, the flight will be on time, and a flight crew will be available.

On one particular fly-out day, Jim Clyburn and I were waiting together at the airport. He asked me how long I'd been married and how I'd met my wife.

"We met at church, Mr. Clyburn," I said. "We met on a church choir tour. How about you and your wife? Where did you two meet?"

"We met in jail, son," he said. "We met in jail."

Jim and Emily Clyburn don't look like a couple who would have ever been in jail, much less have met there. Then again, it wasn't as if the charges were grand theft auto or capital murder. Instead, Jim Clyburn had been arrested, along with nearly four hundred other protesters, after a civil rights march in Orangeburg, South Carolina.

I wasn't born yet during the late 1950s and early 1960s, so the push for civil rights is not something I witnessed firsthand. But Jim Clyburn, as a college student and young working man, lived it. Going to segregated schools is a foreign concept to me. He lived it. Being told you can't eat at a certain restaurant or stay in a certain hotel is foreign to me. He lived it.

There was no bitterness or anger in his voice as Mr. Clyburn told me the story of meeting Miss Emily in jail. He simply wanted me to know that things had not always been as they are now. At a different moment in history, circumstances had led him to join the fight for equality, access, and fairness.

As a student from South Carolina State, he had been part of a planned sit-in at a downtown drugstore, but the protesters had been met with immediate arrest. Emily had come to the jail with another group of students, bringing hamburgers to the hungry protesters and bedsheets to warm up those who had been fire-hosed during the march on that freezing, early-spring day. She shared her hamburger with Jim Clyburn, and that was all it took to catch his eye. They've been married since 1961.

I don't know whether Mr. Clyburn needed to tell his junior colleague the story of how he met his wife, but I do know that I needed to hear it. I wasn't there for any of it, and I can't change a thing about it. But it was entirely appropriate for my heart to break for the past, and I gained a deeper understanding of Congressman Clyburn and his life experience.

TIM

If we want to build friendships with people across lines of division, we must focus on what we have in common and not become distracted by what separates us. We do this naturally—and often without even thinking about it—when we feel a connection with someone. If we want to reach out to people who are different from us, the process is really the same—though we may need to be more *intentional* about it. We must start by establishing rapport, based on common interests, and build a foundation of trust and goodwill, before we gravitate toward conversations about problems and the issues that divide us. If we start by talking about things we can all agree on—such as gratitude for our men and women in uniform, our love for our children, grandchildren, and the Dallas Cowboys (okay, maybe it's not the Cowboys for you, but sports in general)—eventually we will pave the way to more challenging and difficult conversations.

If we're always trying to work an angle rather than establishing a genuine friendship, we'll never get anywhere. But influence and change will come as natural by-products when committed friends work together to address common concerns and interests.

So how do we begin to build friendships across boundaries of division? Let's be honest; we can't just say to someone, "Hey, do you want to be friends?" That would be naive—and more than a little awkward. There's a process I learned while I was running my insurance business, and I believe we can apply these steps to any friendship in our lives.

Start by establishing rapport. When you meet someone new whose perspective on life is different from yours— because of class, race, ethnicity, religion, ideology, or life experience—ask to hear his or her story, and simply start listening. As you listen, put into practice one of the great principles from Stephen Covey's classic bestseller, *The 7 Habits of Highly Effective People*: "Seek first to understand, then to be understood."[5] This is vitally important. Another way to say it is this: *Walk in the other person's shoes for a while before you ask him or her to try on yours.* By doing so, you may expose yourself to a very different way of thinking about and seeing issues. You'll gain a fresh perspective.

Everybody wants to be understood. If you will make "seeking first to understand" a way of life, and if you try to see things from the other person's perspective to the best of your ability, you will find that whenever you walk into a new room, establishing rapport is infinitely easier. When you're willing to enter the situation without preconceived ideas and notions about the other person, then you can start to build rapport. As you interact with each other, actively look for things you have in common and begin to build on those. If differences arise, agree to set them aside in favor of building trust and establishing open lines of communication.

Reaching across lines of division doesn't have to be complicated or difficult. You can start by meeting someone for coffee and having a conversation. You can invite him or her over to your house for dinner. You can go to a high school sporting event together. It doesn't matter so much what you do, as long as you do it together. Take the first step. You'll find that reconciliation and problem-solving will come later.

Begin to build trust and earn credibility. We establish credibility with others by being honest, genuine, and transparent in our communication. If we're honest about where we're coming from, we can often bridge the gap between our differences by increasing our understanding. The more we understand each other, the easier it is to build trust. Credibility is also built on *commitment*—when we're willing to say to the other person, "I'm in your corner, no matter what." That doesn't happen overnight. It takes purpose, patience, and persistence.

Before we can address the issues that divide us, we must first establish credibility in those areas. In politics and in life, we create credibility by doing our homework and becoming proficient on a topic. Credibility is born from our desire to know more about the other person. When we are genuinely interested in understanding other people's perspectives, we will find ourselves able to move quickly and more deeply into relationships with them. In a group, rapport is established through common bonds and core values. These allow for credibility to grow quickly, leading to deeper friendships.

Find a common problem to agree on. Once we have established rapport, trust, and credibility with someone, we may be ready to enter into deeper conversations—to discuss the challenges we face and tackle some of our differences. Trust allows us to identify problems from a common perspective, walk through those problems together, and begin to look for mutually beneficial solutions. The process of building rapport and credibility gives us the understanding of each other we need to work constructively together in an atmosphere of trust and goodwill.

So often, it seems, we look for solutions the wrong way. We put the cart before the horse and try to solve problems that we haven't yet agreed we both have. We can't begin to solve our problems until we've established a common bond and desire to work together. Effective problem-solving can only happen when we've taken the time and put in the effort to establish a genuine and positive working relationship.

It's common in our society to classify people by perceived categories—liberal or conservative, Democrat or Republican, believer or nonbeliever, Northerner or Southerner—and to categorize those groups according to a short list of presumed characteristics that make it easy for us to minimize, attack, or altogether dismiss the group as a whole. But a group is never monolithic; it is always an amalgam of individuals and individual relationships. People don't listen, speak, or respond as a group; they respond as individuals. We may see the crowd, but a crowd is simply a collection of individuals gathered in the same place. Likewise, we don't have relationships with groups; we have relationships with individuals.

Why is this an important distinction?

For one thing, it's easy to hate or demonize a group or a crowd, but it's hard to hate a person whom you've gotten to know. It's easy to cast aspersions on groups, because a group is largely anonymous. Trey and I see the herd mentality all the time when we're speaking in public. If you're facing a crowd, you will hear things that no one would ever say directly to your face. As people, we act differently in groups than we do as individuals.

Interactions with groups almost always go differently than when you invite an individual person into a one-on-one conversation. Connecting with someone one-on-one allows you to go deep and not just wide. It removes any excuses, any barriers.

Sometimes before we can establish rapport, we must confront our own misconceptions. I learned this important lesson from a young woman I met in an airport concourse. It was about six weeks into Donald Trump's presidency, and there were protests left and right. People were stopping me all the time to tell me how unhappy they were with the state of affairs in Washington, DC. I was traveling quite a bit at the time, and one day this young woman stopped me on my way to the departure gate. Everything about her physical appearance told me she was one of those people who didn't like me. Her hair was in dreadlocks, and she had holes in her jeans and a hemp leaf on her shirt. She came right up to me and said, "Senator?"

I was certain she had something negative to say about President Trump and the Republican Party, and I just wanted to walk away. But I was raised with good manners in the South, and thus I told my feet to stand still and my ears to listen to what she had to say. I smiled and replied, "Yes, ma'am."

"Sir, I'm a Democrat, and I didn't vote for you."

"Yes, ma'am," I said. I'm not proud of it, but just by

looking at her, I was pretty sure I knew what she was going to say. I'm just being honest.

"But," she continued, "I've seen what they're saying about you on Twitter."

Her comment put me further on the defensive, because yes, I had just experienced dozens of racially motivated attacks on Twitter. After I announced my support for Senator Jeff Sessions of Alabama as President Trump's choice for attorney general, some folks in the Twittersphere began to question my blackness. They said I had betrayed my race, that I was an Oreo, a white man in a black body. One thing I've learned as a black conservative is that when you challenge the liberal culture and paradigm, you can be seen as challenging black people in general. If you happen to speak up on an issue that is already racially tense—in this case, the senator's background as a white Southerner—you can stir up a hornet's nest of criticism. I had stepped on that hornet's nest and was amply rewarded on Twitter. Now I stood before this young lady, prepared for her to sting me a few more times.

Instead, she said, "I see how people are attacking you. And I just wanted to say . . . well, sir, I hope it isn't one of us."

I was so shocked that my mouth may have actually fallen open. I couldn't have been more surprised if she had told me she was switching her party affiliation. I had judged her, plain and simple, and she had extended grace and empathy to me. I was wrong to prejudge her, and I relearned a valuable lesson.

I thought she wanted to confront me, but instead I was

left to confront my own heart. I landed in a place of judgment because of past experience when people who looked like her had said or done negative things to me. By lumping her into a group, I had failed to see her as an individual. It's always easier to generalize a group than it is to see the individual. I had taken one look at this young woman, and I had drawn my faulty conclusions. That was a real wake-up call for me.

Whether we realize it or not, we tend to impute characteristics to other people, and we view them through the prism of our past relationships. It's hard work to resist the temptation to see a person as part of a group, or as a "type," rather than as an individual. It takes serious effort to be aware of our attitudes and prejudices, and to give people the benefit of the doubt. But dealing with people as individuals is absolutely essential for overcoming stereotypes. Reconciliation requires relationship, and relationship requires fairness and self-awareness.

I can't tell you the number of people who have said to me, "You're the first black person I've ever voted for. You're different from the rest."

I think I understand what they are trying to say. They are working through their own preconceived ideas about me. Here's what I've found: When you begin to look at people as individuals, when you listen to what they say and seek to understand where they're coming from, you begin to realize that we're *all* different from the rest.

Prejudice runs far deeper than skin color or physical

appearance. For example, there was a time in my life when I had too much Christian zeal! I thought all Christians should think the same way I did. It was probably not the most effective way to communicate with people. With time and maturity, I developed a genuine love for other people. That's not to say I'm perfect, by any stretch. I'm still learning. But I've come to appreciate it when someone tells me that I'm "different from the others." Not because it sets me apart, but because it means they have chosen to see me as a person—as an individual—not just as part of a group. My prayer is that they will do this with others as well. If we can make it a habit to see people as individuals, that's half the battle. Once we've opened that door, we're well on our way to establishing rapport, earning trust, and building credibility.

Finally, start to talk about solutions. If we start with something in common and we allow ourselves to bond with others across whatever divisions we may have, the solutions will be a natural by-product of our friendship, our commitment, and our mutual interests. Building rapport requires openness. We have to open our hearts to reach other people.

One thing that happened in Charleston in the aftermath of the shootings at Mother Emanuel Church was a connection between congregations that we hadn't seen before. My church served hundreds of meals during that time, and our pastor reached out to the new pastor at Mother Emanuel, resulting in a positive and potentially powerful friendship that has become life-giving in the community through a renewed commitment to work together.

When you have rapport with someone, you think the best of each other and you give each other the benefit of the doubt. Sadly, too many people too often default to criticizing one another. There's plenty of doubt and suspicion to go around, but there is so much benefit to thinking the best of people. When trust and goodwill dissipate, what's left are people running to their corners—whether that corner is race, ethnicity, religion, political ideology, or some other identity group—and digging in for a fight. But our nation can't afford to splinter into small groups. We need each other to remain strong and to remain free. A persistent focus on our differences and divisions will ultimately lead to the breakdown of what might otherwise be healthy, productive, unifying relationships.

TREY

Part of building rapport is working toward establishing a spirit of reconciliation. Simply stated, reconciliation means a restoration of harmony. Musical harmony is a great metaphor to describe reconciliation because it captures the essential idea of weaving together different notes into a pleasing, cohesive whole. Being in harmony with other people—especially people who are different from us—doesn't mean we have to give up or compromise our values, our history, or our perspectives. It simply means we find ways to blend our distinctive qualities into a unified vision, purpose, or melody. Tim and I believe that reconciliation is possible—and necessary—across all lines of division.

People look to Washington for solutions to our nation's problems, but Congress is often where anger and frustration come home to roost. Although Tim and I are both currently in politics—or perhaps *because* we're in politics—we see the limitations and shortcomings of legislative remedies. We believe the firmest foundation for positive change is found with *individuals* in relationship with one another. Laws are external. Relationships are internal. Policies make you *have* to. Relationships make you *want* to. Relationships contain the power necessary to change the course of history, and the delicate, personal touch needed to change the trajectory of a single life.

TIM

Over the past several years, polls have consistently shown that the majority of Americans feel the country is headed in the wrong direction, and many of these same Americans feel more separated than ever from one another.[6] Clearly, when most of us feel disconnected from our brothers and sisters, we are on the wrong path as a nation.

Differing perspectives are a healthy by-product of a pluralistic society. But when we *divide* over our differences—

retreating to our respective corners—that's when it becomes dangerous and destructive. What still rings true is that when a crisis hits our country, we band together and rapport is almost instantaneous. We saw it after 9/11. We saw it in Charleston after the shootings. We saw it in the nationwide response to Hurricanes Harvey, Irma, Maria, and Nate. In crisis, we do things that are unusual but should be normative. We embrace one another with affection and sincerity because we've been wounded. In times of trouble, we set aside our usual judgments and prejudices and respond to people—not because they are *like* us, but because they are *suffering* like us. But how much better would it be if we would learn how to get along without a major crisis as a catalyst?

TREY

Horrific tragedies such as the bombing of the federal building in Oklahoma City, the attacks on the Twin Towers, or the shooting at the Orlando nightclub can unify people across the nation in a powerful way. The shootings of Representative Gabby Giffords and Representative Steve Scalise instantly unified all members of Congress. But sometimes those feelings of unity begin to dissipate in the weeks and months after a tragedy. We need to capture those fleeting moments of conciliation and goodwill that come so naturally in times of testing, and we need to intentionally embrace unity until it once again becomes part of the fabric of our society on a daily basis. Let unity be what defines us *every* day, not only in response to tragedy.

We're not trying to outline a two-thousand-page government program here. We're simply inviting you to do what we have done: Start a relationship across a line of separation in your life—an intentional relationship trending toward reconciliation. It can be across racial or ethnic lines, religious lines, political or ideological lines—whatever points of division you find in your own community. Or maybe it's reaching into a different community, one you haven't dared to approach before. Listen, learn, strive for understanding, disagree with civility and grace, but most of all, participate in the pursuit of intentional reconciliation.

Tim and I know what has happened in our own lives when we've reached out and shaken hands with people whose appearance, background, perspective, or ideology differs from our own. As we continue to tell our story, perhaps you'll be drawn to look at aspects of your own life. Our fervent hope is to at least challenge you—or better yet, *inspire* you—to take an intentional step in the direction of friendship with someone who seems different from you.

6

Establish Credibility

Creating an Environment Where Trust Can Grow

TIM

On April 4, 2015, my hometown of Charleston, South Carolina, experienced a soul-stirring tragedy that everyone remembers from a cell phone video that went viral. When I say this one hit close to home, I'm not exaggerating. The victim, Walter Scott, and I had the same surname. He was about my age, from my city, and he was shot on a street where I had played as a kid, a street I'd driven for nearly thirty-five years.

The video was heartbreaking to watch. It showed Walter Scott running desperately away from Officer Michael Slager. When Walter was several feet away, the officer opened fire—five, six, seven, eight times. Five of those shots hit Walter, and one proved fatal.

From what can be seen on the video, Walter was hand-cuffed while lying facedown on the ground, but Officer Slager made no attempt to resuscitate him or provide aid. Throughout the incident, the officer appeared unaware that his actions were being recorded.

Within a few days, the eyewitness's cell phone video had provided enough additional evidence for law enforcement to arrest Michael Slager and charge him with murder. Slager's trial began on October 31, 2016, but it ended with a hung jury. Many jurors seemed prepared to convict, but a few wanted to exonerate him.

As a community, we were baffled. It seemed incredible that the case would end in a mistrial. Based on news accounts, the video appeared to show Officer Slager dropping the Taser near Walter Scott's body after he had been shot; and yet there was insufficient evidence to convince all twelve jurors of any crime? To me, that was unbelievable.

TREY

It is one thing to imagine a law enforcement officer shooting a fleeing motorist in the back. It is far more jarring to watch it actually happen on video. But that's what America saw in 2015, after the release of a bystander's cell phone video showed Officer Michael Slager shooting Walter Scott in the back as he attempted to flee.

There was understandable tension in the city of Charleston

as the case worked its way through the legal system. At both state and federal levels, the process demanded and received the attention it deserved. Still, there was a deep uneasiness as yet another racial event affected South Carolina in general and Charleston in particular.

As Tim and I discussed the situation, we felt a growing desire to bring black and white pastors together with black and white police officers, to have the honest dialogue that so often yields understanding and a common purpose. As the tension grew, we wanted to foster conversations and not allow racial incidents to lead to larger racial schisms.

In 2016, after Michael Slager was indicted by a federal grand jury, Tim and I began hosting Pastor/Police Roundtables throughout our state, bringing together pastors, law enforcement officers, and administrators. Our mission was to learn about community relations, interactions between the community and law enforcement, and the similarities and differences among blacks and whites regarding their views of the criminal justice system. Our goal was to provide a safe environment to listen, to vent, to express anger, and to express hope.

We wanted to create a place where real people could express real emotions and do so with an eye toward remedy, understanding, and conciliation. We wanted to cultivate an environment where women and men with a common purpose could meet one another, eat together, talk with honesty, laugh with openness, and disagree with clarity and safety. Still, we were not naive. We know that change doesn't happen overnight or over lunch. But the *desire* for change can happen overnight, and our goal was to establish rapport and create that environment to plant the seeds of trust and credibility.

We started in Columbia, the capital of South Carolina, and we held subsequent gatherings in Greenville and Charleston, usually at a church or in a restaurant. After the initial three meetings were successful, we have continued to host other Roundtables. We have learned so much from these communities and conversations, as they pave the way for honesty across invisible lines. Here are some of the things we've learned from these Roundtables.

Keep cameras and other media out of the meeting. Whenever there are cameras in the room—in any room—people tend to act as if the event is all for show. Cameras signal an ulterior motive, which can have a chilling effect when we are asking people to be open and honest. We knew these meetings required unmitigated candor, so we quickly established the Roundtables as a confidential space, free of cameras or other media. We informed the media about our plans for the meetings, and we were willing to publicly acknowledge what we hoped to accomplish, but there were no cameras and no reporters allowed at our gatherings. Strict confidentiality and complete candor with no fear of judgment or belittlement are essential to our purpose. After all, we all want a safe environment when we are expressing our opinions, explaining our perspectives, and sharing our life experiences.

Trust is foundational. Trust is perhaps the single greatest requirement for any long-term relationship. Once trust is established we can begin to develop a to-do list for how to turn our aspirations into reality. But without mutual trust, and without a deeply held conviction that tangible progress is the most important objective, to-do lists are meaningless.

At our Roundtables, we need the pastors and community leaders to tell the truth about how they view the criminal justice system, and we need the police officers to speak openly about their jobs, their policies and procedures, and their concerns. We need to hear first-person accounts of what it's like to work in the criminal justice system day in and day out. We will learn next to nothing if we must constantly pull our punches or worry about being judged for saying something the wrong way. It's not helpful if both sides aren't willing to talk about how they feel and what they've seen. We're committed to establishing long-term relationships, not just having a onetime chat over lunch and coffee. That requires mutual trust.

We must model vulnerability and commitment. At the Pastor/Police Roundtables, Tim and I hoped to model how two men of different races, with different life experiences and different positions on some of the issues, could have a facts-and-feelings conversation about a variety of important, sensitive issues. We tried to make it clear that the two of us were friends before the Roundtables began, and we would be friends long after the Roundtables ended. Nothing that happened during the Roundtables would change that. Then we tried to draw others into the dialogue with us, emphasizing that not only was it *okay* to have a different perspective, it was actively encouraged. Openness and honesty are expected, laudable, and necessary if we hope to resolve any of the issues at hand.

From our experience at these Roundtable discussions, as well as in bipartisan efforts on Capitol Hill and successful community initiatives at all levels, we've learned that face-to-face personal contact, in a confidential and safe environment, leads to the most open, candid, and useful conversations.

We give each other the benefit of the doubt and work our way through any misunderstandings. The greatest benefit comes from the sheer presence of the other participants. If there were not a common desire to see change and conciliation, none of us would have invested the time and energy to show up for the Roundtable. We may reach similar conclusions or simply agree to disagree, but at least we have opened a dialogue and begun to build trust. Once these dialogues have been established, we are much better prepared to remain in the conversation when the next conflict arises between law enforcement and people in the community.

As we pursue mutually beneficial solutions and outcomes, honesty and candor pave the way. By representing multiple perspectives, the pastors and police officers bring a wider range of ideas to the discussion than either party could have come up with on their own. That mosaic of voices rounds out the full picture.

We can lend our own credibility. Tim and I discovered that when we invested some of the credibility and trust we have with each other within the larger group, we helped to remove barriers between individuals who might not otherwise have been able to get to know each other. Tim did this when he brought his Senate colleague Jeff Sessions to a Roundtable in Charleston shortly after Senator Sessions had been nominated to be attorney general of the United States. When Senator Sessions called Tim to solicit his support and vote during the confirmation process, Tim did something that only he could pull off. He told his colleague, "I don't know whether I can support you or not. But I would like to invite you to Charleston so you can hear some of the concerns I'm hearing, and you can see how important it is to have a top official in the Department of Justice who understands both the greatness and the challenges of our current justice system."

With this invitation, Tim accomplished two things. First, he loaned attorney general nominee Sessions some of his own hard-earned political capital by inviting him to our Roundtable in Charleston. Simultaneously, he let his Senate colleague know that Tim's vote was not guaranteed simply because they were colleagues or from the same political party. Senator Sessions would need to earn that vote by hearing from people directly affected by the decisions made at the highest levels of our justice system.

True to form, the conversation led to an open dialogue among the participants. For his own part, Jeff Sessions came with a willingness to be open to dialogue. He listened more than he talked, which in and of itself sent a signal to those in attendance. I don't know whether anyone's opinion or vote changed that afternoon, but that was not the objective. It wasn't an outcome-driven enterprise, but a process-driven endeavor. It's hard to hate someone you have met in person, shared conversation with, and now know firsthand. It doesn't mean you become a supporter or a lifelong friend, and it doesn't mean you should. But in-person, face-to-face interactions have a humanizing effect on both the speaker and the listener.

Transparency is a powerful tool. I learned this lesson myself when I was a state prosecutor in Upstate South Carolina. I wasn't the attorney general designee for the United States, and I certainly was not a US senator, but the lesson was the same.

The head of the local chapter of the NAACP called our office at the courthouse because he had received a complaint from someone within his community that a white suspect had been treated more leniently than a similarly situated black suspect. The chapter president's approach was professional. He was not accusatory. He simply shared his complaint and asked if I would be willing to discuss the charging decisions with him. I decided to do even better than that: I invited him to our offices at the courthouse.

When he came to see me, I laid the file on a desk and said, "Read it as long as you like, and let's compare notes

afterward." And then I left him alone. He stayed in the conference room for an hour or more, reviewing the file from
beginning to end. And now that he had a firsthand view of
the evidence, he was uniquely equipped to discuss the facts.
I think he was surprised at my willingness to share everything
I could with him. I know I was surprised at his reaction.

He said, "I have a better understanding of why the decision was made, and I am in a position to share this with the
family of the young man involved." Simple, straightforward,
and honest. The next time this same local leader had a question about a case, he called again. This time he did not ask
to see the file. He merely asked if I would summarize the file
for him as best and as fairly as I could. We had established
rapport and a level of trust, and now we were able to build
on that foundation.

Over the course of my time as district attorney, he and I
interacted on a number of cases. He did not always agree with
my decisions, and I did not always agree with his critique of
my decisions. But each of our conversations was private, cen-
tered on the facts, and fair. He brought his concerns to me
directly. We worked our way through the process. I wanted
to make the right decision in all of our criminal cases, and
his perspective and occasional skepticism were elements that
I valued and needed.

I do not expect the president of the local chapter of the
NAACP to ever vote for me. I don't suspect he'll ever ask
me to join his organization. None of that really matters, as
long as we have established a mutual desire to reach the right

decision. I would like to think he picked up a friend along the way. I know I did.

The Pastor/Police Roundtables have proved to be a great way to initiate open and honest conversations between church leaders and law enforcement. This same format could be used to foster communication between people of any opposing sides—police and pastors; Republicans and Democrats; Muslims and Christians; or people with differing views on the death penalty, health care, term limits, the national deficit, or any other issue with the potential to divide us. The possible lines of conflict in our country seem endless. But the opportunities for dialogue and understanding truly *are* endless. Reconciliation can begin with one conversation and one friendship, and it can cross any barrier in existence.

7

A Black Senator's Perspective on Law Enforcement

A Balanced View

TIM

My appreciation for law enforcement goes back many years. I've lived in some very poor areas where crime was rampant, and whenever the police patrolled our area or responded to a situation in the neighborhood, we were grateful. The situation was defused, and the officers were applauded. I remember distinctly the good officers who came to our aid when someone broke into my childhood home. My interactions with law enforcement have been positive and productive. The officers I've known are good people with a strong desire to serve justly. They want to do good, be good, and go home safe after a long shift.

There's no question that the African American community has a long and provocative history with law enforcement. This dates back to the earliest days of our nation, and we've seen a recent spike in aggressive interactions between law enforcement and people of color. We have experienced a level of turmoil not seen in decades, and my heart breaks for us all.

I, too, have had some difficult interactions, on both a personal and professional level. Most African Americans know the meaning of the initials DWB: Driving While Black. During one particular year in my time as an elected official, I was pulled over *seven* times. Was I speeding on one or two of those occasions? Most likely, yes. But the vast majority of times, I was pulled over for driving a new car in the wrong neighborhood, or for some other equally questionable reason. I'm all too familiar with the challenge of Driving While Black.

One time as I was leaving a shopping mall, an officer pulled up right behind me as I pulled out of the parking lot. My senses were immediately on high alert. As I took a left turn out of the mall, I glanced in my rearview mirror. Sure enough, the police car was following me.

I took the second left at a traffic light and turned onto a neighborhood street.

He followed me.

I took the third left onto another street, heading toward my apartment complex.

The police car was right behind me.

Finally, I took a fourth left turn into my apartment complex. *Suddenly, on came the blue lights.*

I immediately pulled to the side and waited for the officer to approach my vehicle. If you've ever been pulled over, you know the anxiety. He asked for my license and registration, and then he said, "You didn't use your turn signal on that last turn."

Keep in mind, the officer had been on my tail ever since I left my parking space at the mall. I had watched in my rear-view mirror as he followed me all the way home. It's possible that I'm sometimes careless about using my turn signal, but do you really think I failed to signal when I knew I was under such scrutiny? As someone who has been pulled over more times than I can remember, I knew by the fact that he had been following me for so long that he was looking for a reason to flip on the lights. I can tell you without a doubt that I signaled all my turns that day. But there I sat, pulled over, at the mercy of an officer who was accusing me of something I was certain I hadn't done.

Another time, I was following a friend to a restaurant for dinner. As soon as we pulled out onto the road, there were flashing blue lights in my rearview mirror. The officer pulled me over to the median, and we went through the usual drill with the license and registration. This time, the officer just wanted to make sure that my car wasn't a stolen vehicle. Questions flooded my mind: *Is the license plate on record as stolen? Does the license plate not match the car? Is there any logic to why this is happening?*

After fifteen minutes or so, he was satisfied and let me go.

Of course, I'm not the only black motorist to experience situations like these. In fact, I don't know many black men who *don't* have a story like one of these. It's no small thing for a black person to be pulled over, for *any* reason. It happens every day, all across the country, whether we want to admit it or not. My brother—now a retired command sergeant major in the US Army, the highest rank for an enlisted soldier—was pulled over while driving from Texas to Charleston early in his career. The officer just wanted to confirm that the car my brother was driving, his Volvo, was indeed his own. One of my former staffers used to drive a Chrysler 300—a nice car, to be sure. But he was pulled over so many times, for absolutely no reason other than that he was a black man driving a nice car, that he finally decided it might be time to buy some different wheels.

I have been the target of racial profiling even as a public servant. Prior to my election to Congress, I held office at the county and state levels. As an elected official, I believe it is my responsibility to get out among my constituents and hear their concerns, so I accepted an invitation to an out-of-town event. I traveled with two of my staff members and two police officers. Everyone in our group was white, except me.

When we arrived, my two staffers walked into the building along with the two officers, and everything was just fine. But when I got to the door, the greeter was suddenly not so fine with letting me in. The two police officers who were with me were outraged by this exclusion, and their utter disbelief was a blessing to me. Their support for me, and their willingness to stand up and say, "This is not right!" is the best memory of that day. Otherwise, it's another incident I would love to forget.

Surprisingly, I have even experienced racial profiling on Capitol Hill. Keep in mind that I'm one of the easier senators to recognize, given that I was the only black member of the Senate at the time I was appointed. Members of Congress have a few ways we can identify ourselves when we enter the Capitol, including ID badges and a lapel pin. But after we've been here for a year or two, most Capitol Police officers simply recognize us.

In 2015, almost five years into my government service, I entered one of the congressional buildings with my lapel pin on. As I walked in, the security officer stopped me and said, "I recognize the pin, but I don't recognize you."

So what are you trying to say? I thought to myself. *Either you think I'm committing a crime by impersonating a member of Congress or . . . what?*

He asked to see my ID, and of course I showed it to him, but why should I have had to? Later that evening, I received a call from a Capitol Police supervisor, apologizing for the incident—the third such call I had received in the past year or so.

Thankfully, I have not endured bodily harm at the hands of the police, unlike others, but I have felt the pressure that is applied by the scales of justice when they are askew. I have felt the anger, frustration, sadness, and humiliation that come with feeling as if you've been targeted for nothing more than being yourself.

The former staffer I mentioned, the one who sold his Chrysler 300, expressed the frustration so well: "There are few things more damaging to the soul than to know you're following the rules and being treated as if you're not."

Situations like the ones I've described may not happen a thousand times a day, but they happen far too often. Speaking from experience, I can say they are not easily forgotten. It's humiliating to be falsely accused. It makes a person feel small. And it can be dangerous when the one accusing you is in a position of authority. To view someone as guilty by association— simply because of race, religion, or nationality—is demeaning and detrimental to our democracy. Incidents like these have caused a deep divide between people of color and law enforcement in many cities and towns across the nation. There is a trust gap, a tension, that has been growing for decades. Tragically, some incidents *have* ended in bodily harm, or even death. We're all too familiar with those.

African Americans are often disappointed with the justice system. They feel as if Lady Justice is holding scales that are out of balance. Lady Justice may be the only part of the legal system that is truly blind; it seems too many people involved notice skin color much more than we would like. When you can lose your freedom—or your life—over unfairness in the justice system, it undermines the rule of law and our basic human dignity in a most critical part of the American landscape.

Still, police officers are a central part of our American family. Our nation is dependent on the rule of law, and we need honest, hardworking men and women to take up the shield. Police officers are men and women who see their job as a calling. They have two goals: to protect and serve. What will we do if they stop policing? Who will we call for help? We cannot allow the actions of a few to overwhelm the good of the majority, especially when so many do it so well. Let's focus on the fact that most law enforcement officers are true American heroes. It's hard to imagine putting your life on the line for people you've never met, yet they do it willingly, day in and day out. That's a ministry, actually. I like to think of police officers as ministers to society. It gives me great joy when I get to call someone in uniform with praise or con-gratulations. I am personally thankful for specific members of law enforcement who have been willing to stand with me during some very difficult times.

Yes, I have some questions and hesitations about decisions that a minority of law enforcement officers have made, but that is only part of the picture. I've been on enough ride-alongs to know the danger they face in their world, and I will never try to minimize that. It's precisely because I have so much respect for law enforcement as a whole that when they disappoint, especially when they misuse the authority of the badge, it is profoundly discouraging and frustrating. Along with that formal authority there must be a well-earned moral authority.

The same is true for Trey and me and our colleagues in

Washington. If we seek positions of leadership—as elected officials or as law enforcement officers—we should expect scrutiny of our actions. Analysis and inquiry are necessary for good leadership and good public service.

TREY

As a nation, we have lived with the consequences of racial disharmony for a long time, and I think most of us would just as soon not have to think about it. We have consciously avoided the issue of race because it is so personal and its roots go so deep in our history. It is painful. It can be consuming and divisive. It can be a conversation stopper, when what we desperately need is to start the conversation in a different way.

Avoiding the issue has not and will not make it disappear. We need to talk about it. We need to ask people why they believe what they believe. If we don't like all the suspicion and blame, we need to give people a reason to trust. Let's be honest about our experiences. If you're a police officer, you can easily explain why there is no such thing as a "routine traffic stop." You can explain why the very word *routine* trivializes the daily risks of your job. You can explain what it feels like to wear a firearm for personal protection every single day. You can share some of the names you are called simply because you are wearing the uniform you have been assigned to wear.

If you're a black person with a car and a driver's license, you can best explain why the fear of Driving While Black rides with you everywhere you go. It isn't confined to isolated incidents. It can even affect a US senator. You can explain what it feels like to view the police as a force to avoid rather than a force to embrace. You can explain how it feels when the response time is slower to your neighborhood than to one across town.

As the conversation progresses, you may begin to see that you both view the situation precisely the same way, even though your nomenclature may be different. We want the same things, and we'll begin to realize that as soon as we become willing to *listen* to each other, to look at life through the prism of someone else's point of view.

At a recent Pastor/Police Roundtable where we discussed the shooting of Walter Scott, one of the black pastors said that as soon as he heard the racial composition of the jury—eleven white jurors and one black juror—he "knew the verdict would be not guilty." He said he knew there was no way eleven white jurors would find a white man guilty of shooting a black man. He immediately assumed the verdict would not speak the truth.

I have spent a lot of time in courtrooms, standing up for victims of color in front of both white and black jurors. I've worked with countless women and men of color in uniform who have dedicated their careers to making that kind of conclusion obsolete. What made this pastor an expert on juries?

I didn't know whether to be angry or shocked, so I made

the intentional decision to be neither. Instead, I asked him with genuine interest, "What in your experience led you to that conclusion?" It turned out to be a lot of things. Clearly, it would serve no purpose to question or cross-examine his life experience, which was more immediate and more real to him than any anecdote I might share or any set of statistics I could locate.

My question, and his response, led to a discussion about the nature of juries and how they are selected—or rather, *un*selected. You don't pick juries; you unpick them. Starting with a randomly assembled group of thirty or so people, the prosecution and the defense begin to "strike" or whittle the larger group down to twelve who will hear the case. It isn't so much that the twelve jurors who are left are agreeable or wholly acceptable to both the prosecution and the defense; it's more that the ones who were struck were *un*acceptable to one side or the other.

There are two ways to strike potential jurors. Obviously, you can strike a juror "for cause" if he or she knows one of the witnesses, recently suffered from a strikingly similar crime, or otherwise indicates that he or she cannot decide the case fairly. Those are easy decisions. In addition, each side is allowed a certain number of "peremptory strikes," which means a potential juror can be removed without a specific, detailed reason. For example, maybe you don't want psychologists or dentists on your jury for some reason. Maybe you don't like the sports team on a person's T-shirt. You will have your reasons, but the point is you don't have to state them to the court.

There are two exceptions to the peremptory challenge: You cannot strike a potential juror on the basis of race or gender. The Supreme Court made this clear in *Batson v. Kentucky* (1986) about race, and in *J.E.B. v. Alabama* (1994) about gender.

I fundamentally did not agree with the pastor at that Roundtable, because I have witnessed firsthand when mostly or entirely white juries decided in favor of a black victim. I've also seen death penalty cases with a disproportionate number of black jurors (relative to the population ratios in the community) sentence defendants to death based in part on law enforcement testimony. But the purpose of these Roundtable conversations is to create a safe place for both pastors and police to speak freely and vulnerably, not to debate the social science behind *Batson v. Kentucky*.

The truth is, that pastor was sharing from his own experience, from what he had witnessed, and it wasn't my place to disagree with his life experience. In fact, these are precisely the kinds of frank, raw, and candid conversations we need to have with one another. It hurt to hear his candor, but I appreciated it. I'm sure it was painful for the black police officers who were present, as well. But it was his perspective—and ignoring it or wishing that what he shared wasn't prevalent wouldn't have changed a thing. Those of us at the Roundtable that day needed to hear that pastor's raw words, to see things from his perspective, and to understand what he believed and why.

In reference to the Walter Scott case, he felt justified in

his belief—at least initially. After all, there was a hung jury, which means the jurors could not reach a unanimous verdict, even with the video evidence. The pastor believed that the jury wouldn't convict a white man, but in fact the jury could not decide either way.

As a prosecutor, I struggle to explain what happened in that case, though I am grateful that people trust me enough to ask me to explain it. I know the prosecutor who was assigned to that case. She is a talented trial attorney, with a background in both the federal and state criminal justice systems. I haven't talked to her about the case, and I did not watch the trial. I do not have all the facts. I did not review all the evidence, and I did not sit through the entire trial. But I do know that the hung jury was a tremendous disappointment to those following the case. It is difficult to imagine what evidence is necessary if a video recording is insufficient.

Though there is much about this trial I can't explain, here's what I do know for sure: When the mistrial was declared, there were no riots in Charleston. Nobody pillaged the streets or set things on fire. People did not hurt other innocent people because of what they perceived to be an incorrect court verdict. Though many people remain bitterly disappointed, they did not resort to violence to show their displeasure. It was a tremendous testimony to the goodness of the people of Charleston and South Carolina. It was a testimony to how far we've come in our desire to live in peace.

It is also a testimony to the fact that, whether black or white, we can all grieve the loss of a black man's life at the hands of a law enforcement officer. And as we saw with the shootings at Mother Emanuel Church, both black and white can grieve the loss of good people who were killed after inviting a stranger to open the Bible with them. Hopefully, the lines of demarcation are beginning to fade.

Tim has heard me say this a million times, but it's because I believe it wholeheartedly: We desperately need a justice system that is respected by all and worthy of respect by all. Those are two different objectives, both of which are essential to the community we want to live in. To the extent we are wired to need any line of division in our culture, let that line be simply this: people of good conscience versus people who seek to do harm. No other lines are necessary. Those of us who want to live in a culture brimming with fairness, security, equality, and proportionality are united together on one side, regardless of any other characteristics we have. Our common bond is simply one of good conscience.

8

A White Former Prosecutor's Perspective on Law Enforcement

To Pursue the Truth

TREY

When I was growing up, my father would not allow my sisters or me to use the word *cop*. He felt it was disrespectful. He insisted on the terms *police* or *law enforcement*.

The respect for law enforcement instilled in me by my father continues to this day in large and small ways. I do not listen to music that refers to police officers in derogatory terms, and my children do not listen to that music either (at least not around me). At public events, I always make it a point to speak to the police officers there. And on those occasions when I am driving faster than I should and I see a police officer turn around or activate the blue lights, I do not wait for the officer to pull in behind me or turn on the sirens. I pull over immediately.

I know police officers are just as capable of being flawed as the rest of us, and I have worked with some, prosecuted some, and referred others for discipline—those who were a real discredit to their line of work. Still, I have met far more good officers than bad, and I am still prone to bias in favor of law enforcement. Although I will confess that initial bias, it doesn't mean I lack the objectivity to view facts fairly. It simply means I view law enforcement as a symbol of fairness, a line between people of good conscience and those who would take advantage. And I am keenly aware of the challenges, practical and otherwise, that law enforcement officers face on a daily basis.

When did we as a society begin to lose respect for those who are charged with keeping the peace and protecting us? And how do we recapture that respect as a point of unity? How do we recapture the marvel that women and men are willing to wear a uniform, a badge, and a gun to keep others safe—including those who may not respect them or their uniform?

Tim and I have different perspectives on law enforcement, as one might expect, given our different life experiences. He was a business owner and a regular citizen, while I was on the inside of the criminal justice system as a prosecuting attorney. I worked with police officers on a daily basis for nearly two decades. My perspective is informed and instructed by the women and men with whom I worked. There were a few bad apples in the bunch, but the overwhelming majority were conscientious, hardworking, and devoted to order, structure, and safety. Most of the officers I worked with were husbands and wives, fathers and mothers, who wanted the same things out of life that we all want: to protect and provide for those they love. Police officers do not make much money. They often work more than one job, and their families sacrifice and struggle because of the long and difficult hours. Those are the images that inform and instruct my view of law enforcement, punctuated by the stories of individuals who stand out the most—individuals like Kevin Carper.

Kevin was a uniformed patrol officer with the Spartanburg County Sheriff's Office. Patrol officers are the ones who initially respond to a crime scene or an incident. They are dispatched by the 9-1-1 operator when someone calls for help.

Kevin and his partner were working their usual shift one evening when they received a call to respond to a domestic violence incident in progress. There is nothing routine about domestic violence calls. They are often dangerous—and potentially lethal—for the victim, the perpetrator, and the officers involved.

On this particular night, Kevin and his partner arrived to find William Seich pointing a gun at his girlfriend, Patricia Parris. Parris was crouched down in the front yard, trying to shield herself behind a tree, and one of her daughters was nearby. Seich was on the small front porch of their mobile home, holding a large-caliber handgun.

When the officers arrived on scene, they had to make a split-second decision.

Is the gun real? Is the gun loaded? Do we shoot the gunman? Do we have a clear line of fire? Is there any chance of endangering others?

William Seich's gun was real, and it was loaded. Before the deputies could intervene, he used it to shoot his girlfriend to death. When he turned and pointed the gun at Kevin and his partner, they both fired their service weapons toward the front porch. Unbeknownst to the deputies, Parris's other daughter was inside the mobile home, and she was struck by a bullet from one of the officers' guns.

William Seich survived to be charged with the murder of his girlfriend. Both girls survived, though one was badly injured.

I met Kevin Carper as we were gearing up for trial. He was an essential witness, and I needed to prepare him for what would be a grueling cross-examination. He would be second-guessed, and his every move would be scrutinized. The defense would try to blame Kevin for Patricia's murder, saying he didn't do enough, didn't do it soon enough, and didn't make wise decisions. These are judgments reached with the clarity of hindsight, but such are the challenges facing a sheriff's deputy on a domestic violence call. This is what officers have to endure in courtrooms all across the country on a daily basis: cross-examination by defense attorneys who have the benefit of hindsight.

As Kevin and I talked, it was clear to me that his mind

and heart were somewhere else. Finally, I said, "Kevin, there is nothing you could have done. It was William Seich who killed his girlfriend, not you."

"I know, Solicitor Gowdy," he replied, "but we shot that little girl." Tears streamed down his face. "We shot that little girl!"

Objectively, Kevin Carper did everything right. He responded to an incredibly tense domestic call. He was confronted with an armed man who was threatening a woman, and he had only a few seconds to make life-and-death decisions.

Still, it didn't matter how many times I told Kevin he had done the right thing. It didn't matter how many times I tried to reassure him there was no way he could have known about the girl inside the mobile home. Honestly, Kevin and his partner may have saved both girls' lives by showing up as quickly as they did. But all Kevin could see was that an innocent girl had been struck and badly injured by a bullet from a law enforcement officer's gun.

During the trial, Kevin Carper was a remarkable witness, unafraid to show his humanity and compassion, even while being cross-examined by the criminal defense attorney about his alleged investigative shortcomings. In the end, William Seich was convicted of murder and sentenced to life in prison.

Kevin Carper was a fantastic law enforcement officer with a bright future ahead of him. He was precisely the kind of person we want and need in law enforcement. I meant to tell him that after the jury returned their verdict. But in South

Carolina state criminal court, the sentencing takes place immediately after the guilty verdict is returned by the jury. The jury is polled, the sentencing sheets must be completed, and the family and friends of the victim are given a chance to address the judge. It's a hectic time in the aftermath of a jury trial.

I meant to tell Kevin what a great witness he had been. I meant to tell him how captivated the jury was by his testimony and demeanor. I meant to tell him he had handled the incident, the aftermath, and the trial preparation with admirable professionalism. I meant to tell him how beautifully the law and humanity intersected in his testimony; how encouraging it was to see a courageous man who knew he had made the right decision and yet still grieved over the unintended consequences of that decision because innocent people had been affected. After all, isn't that the society we want to live in: the one where the law intersects with humanity and grace? I meant to tell him all of that, but he slipped out of the courtroom while I was preparing for the sentencing.

I'll tell him the next time I see him, I thought. He was an excellent officer, and I knew he would one day testify at another trial.

The next time I saw Kevin Carper, he was lying beside the road near some woods on the western side of Spartanburg County. He had been shot to death as he tried to apprehend a man with more than thirty previous arrests and convictions. Kevin was killed as he tried to effect another "routine" traffic stop. He left a young widow and three small children.

The finality of the officer's death hit the hardest at the end of the graveside service, when a final radio transmission was played.

"Deputy Kevin Carper, this is dispatch. Do you copy?"

"Deputy Kevin Carper, this is dispatch. Do you copy?"

"Deputy Kevin Carper, this is dispatch. Your shift is over. You are cleared to go home."

John Adams was right when he said we are a nation of laws, not men. But a nation that respects the law must also respect those who dedicate their lives to the execution and enforcement of the law. What makes us a great people is the compassion that fills in the gaps left by the cool impartiality of the law. The law enforcement officers I worked with the most knew when to combine the law with humanity to produce *justice*.

If you want to know why I respect and appreciate law enforcement so much, it's because I know there are people like Kevin Carper dedicating their lives to protect and serve their communities. We shouldn't wait until the funeral, when it's too late to let them know how much we appreciate them. We honor them as we produce, create, and re-create a justice system befitting their service.

Police officers are charged with maintaining law and order and protecting public safety. For me, as a former prosecutor, that means we preserve order, structure, stability, and security in our society by upholding the rule of law. But as I was preparing for a Pastor/Police Roundtable in Greenville, something told me that others might have a different understanding.

When I asked the participants what came to mind when they heard "law and order" and "public safety," a young black pastor was candid enough to speak up.

"I hear code talk," he said. "I hear, 'Lock up people of color' or 'Lock up young black males.'"

Wow. I appreciated his honesty, which got me thinking about the importance of defining our terms, being sensitive to what other people hear when we speak, and coming to a mutual understanding in our efforts to bridge the gap between what we say, what we mean, and what others think we mean when they hear our words.

When I use the phrase "law and order," I'm drawing a distinction between people of good conscience and people who are criminally inclined. It has nothing to do with race. It applies as equally to someone like William Seich, a middle-aged white male, as it would to anyone else who breaks the law.

Every person of good conscience wants peace and security. To me, "law and order" does not mean "Let's lock 'em all up." It means "Let's keep everyone safe. Let's keep all people of good conscience safe."

When I speak, the intention behind my words is important; but what the other person *hears* is even more important. The quality of any communication is always determined by the listener. Unless the other person understands and receives what we meant to say, we haven't communicated effectively. We must speak the same language, define our terms, pursue a common understanding, and be bold and honest enough to speak up with one another, as that young pastor did with me. It doesn't have to be confrontational—in fact, it's better if it's not—but it must be candid, truthful, and to the point. And we must be willing to listen and seek to understand the other side's perspective.

TIM

Many older African Americans live in neighborhoods that have deteriorated. Young families in these same neighborhoods want their kids to be able to play on safe streets. Every family wants to live in a place where "law and order" is a positive term.

But historically speaking, the phrase "law and order" has felt like a threat to the freedom of black people. Many of us are old enough to remember a guy with a bullhorn or a fire hose. We picture somebody wanting to forcibly remove us and lock us all up. When anyone says that "stop and frisk" policies are not unconstitutional, it feels unsettling to me. It feels alarming to think that someone has legal authorization to stop and frisk me, based on a *hunch* and nothing else. That's terrifying to people who have experienced a loss of freedom because of someone else's abuse of power.

There are phrases and word choices that can evoke a sense of danger, even in someone who is comfortable with law enforcement and supportive of police officers. That sense of danger only becomes more real when policies are put in place to make those dangers *legal*.

TREY

If we didn't live in such a racialized world, we wouldn't have the same concerns about "stop and frisk." We'd be more likely to see the world as two kinds of people: law-abiding and law-breaking. But of course we do live in a racialized world, and sometimes a person's color, race, or ethnicity can take precedence over seemingly everything else. It might be helpful for us to take a step back and look at the concept of fairness in the law.

There are two kinds of discrimination: intentional discrimination and discrimination in application. The law makes a distinction between *de jure* and *de facto* discrimination. At face value, the law applies equally across the board, regardless of race; but in its application, it plays out differently. Our drug laws are a perfect example of the difference.

When I worked at the US Attorney's office, from 1994 to 2000, possession of *500 grams* of powder cocaine would result in a mandatory minimum prison sentence of five years. That was a race-neutral standard; it applied to everyone. At the same time, possession of only *5 grams* of cocaine base, or what is commonly called crack cocaine, would result in the same mandatory minimum five years in prison. Again, a race-neutral standard based on the amount of the controlled substance one had in his or her possession. So at face value, the law was neutral. But it was not at all neutral in its application—for one simple reason: Powder cocaine was the drug of choice primarily for white defendants, whereas crack cocaine was more likely the drug of choice for black defendants. So you have to wonder: Is there a race-neutral reason for a 100:1 disparity in the amount of narcotics possession for the same sentence? Even if the intention behind the disparity was completely neutral—and you're free to decide that for yourself—the net effect of the law was *de facto* discriminatory.

It should be noted that the 100:1 ratio was reduced to 18:1 (500 grams of powder cocaine compared to 28 grams of crack) by the Fair Sentencing Act of 2010. This reduced the sentencing disparity but did not eliminate it. And the underlying questions still remain.

We need to open up conversations like this one, to talk about the various perspectives on this law. One could certainly argue, "Well, you shouldn't be selling drugs." That's true, but it's not the end of the analysis. If people *are* selling drugs, which they are doing, why not punish them equally? Why not have equal sentencing standards, whether the drug is heroin, crack cocaine, or methamphetamine?

Let's at least acknowledge the tragic truth that a generation of young black men have received longer prison sentences than their white counterparts because they possessed a less-expensive form of the same drug—the only real difference being the addition of baking soda, which most of us have in our kitchens.

I have talked to hundreds of young black men who were sentenced to lengthy prison terms for possession of cocaine base with intent to distribute. Clearly, these young men did something wrong, and I was the one who prosecuted them. But most of them, I suspect, will learn nothing in the twentieth year of their incarceration that they could not have learned in five.

These are not violent criminals. These are young men who made terrible decisions to sell terrible products, chiefly for financial gain. They deserve to be punished. But in terms of proportionality and fundamental fairness, many of them do not deserve the length of sentences they received.

I remember walking out of a federal courtroom in Anderson, South Carolina, in the late 1990s after a young man I prosecuted received a lengthy sentence for conspiracy to possess cocaine base with intent to distribute. As I opened the door to my truck, I thought of my friend Tommy Pope, who prosecuted Susan Smith, the South Carolina woman who drowned her two young sons in 1994 by strapping them into their car seats and allowing the car to roll into a Union County lake. That premeditated murder remains one of the most disturbing crimes ever committed in South Carolina. I thought of that case as I got into my truck because Susan Smith will be eligible for parole before the man I convicted for possession of crack cocaine. Justice has to include proportionality. In those cases, it did not.

If only we could go back to the earliest conversations about these laws. If only we could be certain that racial motives were not part of the conversation. If only we could start the discussion with our mutual desire to live in a safe environment.

In the long term, I think the only thing we'll have left is a respect for the law in its equal application. When that begins to erode, we're finished. I don't mean to sound apocalyptic, but I don't see how we can survive in a world where law, procedure, and due process don't matter. That is my selfish motive for wanting people whose perspective differs from mine to tell me the truth about their experience with the criminal justice system. Let's see if we can fix it. Let's see if we can build a justice system that is fully respected and fully worthy of respect. Let's see if we can move toward that simple dichotomy between people who are of good conscience and people who aren't.

TIM

The introduction of body cameras and dash cams for police officers, the proliferation of smartphones that put a video recorder in everyone's pocket, and the relative ease of uploading content onto the Internet have allowed the nation and the world to witness some tragic interactions between the police and people of color over the past several years. But that's not because the tenuous and sometimes explosive relationship between law enforcement and the African American community in particular is a new phenomenon. Sadly, decades of frustration, mistrust, and misunderstanding have brought us to this point. Technology has only made it more visible to a wider audience.

We cannot allow violence to overtake the soul of a movement for justice. I truly believe that, in our nation, peaceful protest is the only effective way to achieve social change.

For me, the issue boils down to two major points: All lives must matter equally in the eyes of the justice system and law enforcement, and we must focus on inner-city crime, not just on black interactions with law enforcement. A disproportionate number of homicides nationwide occur in just a handful of cities, including Chicago, Philadelphia, Detroit, and Washington, DC. The innocent lives that are lost in these cities are precious and should demand our attention.

TREY

As a former prosecutor, let me tell you one of my worst-case scenarios. You have a violent crime involving a black assailant and a black victim. There are witnesses to the crime. There are people who could help the police make a case against the perpetrator, but no one comes forward. The district attorney needs those witnesses to cooperate, or there's no way to move ahead with an arrest and prosecution.

When witnesses don't cooperate with the police, it has the effect of devaluing the victim. The district attorney cannot pursue justice without witnesses. If people won't come forward because they don't trust the police, the prosecution will never be fully successful.

It's almost a self-perpetuating downward spiral. Some people believe that black victims are treated differently and are somehow devalued by the justice system. But the value of any case is directly proportional to the evidence the prosecutor can acquire and present. If witnesses withhold information or don't come forward, it ends up hurting the victim by making the case more difficult or even impossible to prosecute. I saw this cycle repeat itself time and time again when I was a prosecutor.

I've had this conversation a thousand times with black leaders. I worked with Tony Fisher, the chief of police in Spartanburg, who was trying to ensure *justice for all* in his jurisdiction. Together, we implored other community leaders, "Your failure to cooperate with us is what devalues the lives of the very people you want to help. We need people who are willing to say, 'Yes, I was there.' 'Yes, I saw what he did.' 'Yes, I saw the car that drove by and shot up the outdoor party.'" It is illogical and unhelpful to know there were thirty people at a party and yet believe that not a single one saw the car that drove by and opened fire.

The justice system needs the witnesses, the victims need the witnesses, and our broader community needs the witnesses. Trust is part of the foundation for building a cohesive community. But when I can't fully and effectively prosecute the crimes committed against victims of color, it has the perverse effect of devaluing the lives of the very people we are trying to value equally.

TIM

Sometimes witnesses don't come forward to testify because they are afraid of retribution by the people who committed the crime. It's not always that they don't trust the police. Still, we need a more holistic approach. Everyone who jeopardizes a life should be held to the same standard. How people in authority wield that authority should be a serious concern of ours because it can slant the scales of justice. But that's only part of the problem and not the main focus.

I believe we should put a premium on *all* life, from conception to the grave, and stop dividing our nation into subgroups. We've already had too much of that. I'm not opposed to emphasizing specific issues within our communities, but I choose not to intentionally segregate myself in order to make progress. I'm going to intentionally *include* myself instead. We're all in this together.

9

The Power of a Positive Influence

The Impact of a Sunday School Teacher
and a Businessman

TREY

Throughout most of this book, the type of friendship we've focused on has been like that of David and Jonathan—the kind of friend who will stick with you through thick and thin, who looks out for your best interests and has your back.[7] To that essential foundation, we would add the idea of iron sharpening iron—the kind of friend who hones you and makes you a better person.[8]

When I reflect on the iron-sharpening metaphor, one picture that comes to mind is that of sparks flying as "mettle meets mettle." This would certainly apply to *unlikely* friendships, where our differences provide ample opportunity for conflict. Whenever we reach across lines of division and engage with people who are different in some significant way, there's bound to be friction—a clashing of swords, so to speak. But the Bible suggests that iron on iron is *good*, because it makes us both sharper, more fit for the task at hand, whatever that task may be.[9]

I think it's important to have a colleague or a peer who will help to keep you sharp, but as you think about ways to engage with people despite your differences, don't overlook opportunities for unlikely friendships based on differences of age and experience. *Mentoring* relationships are some of the most productive, powerful, and satisfying friendships we can have.

This, too, has a biblical basis. Jesus and his disciples, the apostle Paul with Timothy and Titus, and Elijah with Elisha—all are powerful examples the Bible gives us of mentoring relationships. As Tim and I look back on our growing-up years, we can both attest to the life-changing, life-defining influence of a mentor at key times in our lives.

I remember one afternoon when I was in eighth grade. I was in the basement, watching professional wrestling on television with my two younger sisters—over their strenuous objections—when my mom called down the stairs.

"Trey, Dick Littlejohn is on the phone for you."

Oh, this can't be good, I thought.

Dick Littlejohn was the owner of a chain of grocery stores called Community Cash. They were closed on Sundays and did not sell beer, wine, or liquor. In its prime, Community

Cash had between thirty-five and forty grocery stores across Upstate South Carolina, providing employment to hundreds of men and women. These were neighborhood stores where Saturday shopping was about more than just groceries—it was the weekly social event.

Mr. Littlejohn was married to a beautiful woman named Margaret. She had survived polio, breast cancer, and an acoustic neuroma, all with extraordinary grace and class. The Littlejohns had two children, Rick and Ann. Rick was a little older than I was; Ann was a little younger.

Mr. Littlejohn was also my eighth grade Sunday school teacher—which was why my heart sank when I heard he was on the phone. You see, I was terrible in Sunday school. Really bad. I wasn't malicious or mean spirited. I just could not stop talking. So when Mr. Littlejohn called me at home, my first thought was, *What have I done wrong this time?*

I could not remember any specific infraction, but my mind and heart were racing as I walked toward the phone. Mr. Littlejohn had unconventional ways of teaching Sunday school. He gave silver dollars for each Bible verse memorized—and yes, "Jesus wept" counted. Most of the verses I still know today are because Mr. Littlejohn gave me an incentive to learn them. His approach was a bit unusual, but it worked—like just about every unconventional thing Mr. Littlejohn tried during his long and productive life.

When I picked up the phone, he said, "Son, I'm going to Washington, DC, by train. And I wonder if you would go with me."

At first, I was relieved that I wasn't in trouble. But I wasn't exactly ready to go on a long-distance trip with my Sunday school teacher.

"Well . . . ," I stammered, "I have to ask my mom and dad."

"Of course you do," he said. "You go talk to them, and I will talk to them, and let's see if this is something you want to do."

My parents were already very familiar with Mr. Littlejohn. He was highly respected in our church and was known for his generosity, his commitment to our youth ministry, and his willingness to sacrifice financially in the business realm to abide by his spiritual convictions. My father and Mr. Littlejohn served on the deacon board together, and my mother and Mrs. Littlejohn were friends.

I went upstairs and told my mom, "Mr. Littlejohn just invited me to go with him to Washington, DC, but I don't want to go."

I thought she would understand the discomfort and reluctance of a thirteen-year-old boy to travel with his Sunday school teacher. I figured she would do what she had always done for me in life: bail me out and not mention a word to my father. Instead, she said, "I think that's a great idea. He's a wonderful man with a beautiful family who has done so much for our community and our church. It will be a good experience for you."

Gee, thanks, Mom.

A few days later, Mr. Littlejohn and I boarded the train in Spartanburg, and I quickly discovered that traveling with him was very different from traveling with my own family. I never knew that people actually ordered steak for breakfast, until Mr. Littlejohn did it on the train to Washington. In DC, I ate filet mignon for the first time, and when he saw how much I liked it, he called the waiter over to our table and said, "Bring him another one." My father had us kids ordering off the children's menu until the 365th day of the last year we were eligible, so eating a double portion of filet mignon was an eye-opening experience, to say the least.

Mr. Littlejohn and my father had both worked hard for everything they had, but my dad had grown up in more challenging circumstances, and he practiced all the frugality you would expect from a man who knew what it meant to be poor. He delivered newspapers to pay for college, and after taking all the math and science classes he could, he made the most of his limited resources by leaving before graduating to enroll in medical school. (Back then, you could do things like that.) Among the many things I learned from my father were order, self-discipline, and the value of a good education.

By the time I was in junior high, my father was a well-established, well-respected, and successful physician, and he still saved everything he could. He did not waste things, because there had been nothing to waste when he was my age.

My mother also grew up poor, but because she lived in the country, she said she never realized she was poor. She thought all little girls' dresses were made from feed sacks and their dolls made from corn husks. In spite of these circumstances (or perhaps because of them), my parents have lived significant lives that have had a positive impact on everyone who has come into contact with them.

My parents appreciated Mr. Littlejohn's commitment to young people, and they appreciated his ability to travel and his willingness to take me and others along with him. As a pediatrician, my dad worked very long hours and was often on call. Besides, if he had taken me on a trip to New York or Washington, he would have also taken my mother and my three sisters—and none of us wanted to spend our family vacation on a historical tour of Washington, DC.

My parents understood that sometimes a young person needs to hear things from someone outside the family—a lesson I have applied with my own children. With my parents' blessing and encouragement, I was fortunate to be introduced to a different perspective on life by Mr. Littlejohn.

That trip to Washington was the first of many he and I would take together. He took me to Africa so I could see a different culture, but he also wanted me to experience the abject poverty that was pervasive in Ethiopia. He took me to Israel, where he wanted me to meet some of the young Palestinian boys who were begging for money from the tourists. There I was able to see how a person could be made to feel less than human.

"This is where you learn to hate, son" was all that Mr. Littlejohn would say about it. He knew that *seeing* how such humiliation taught these young Arab and Palestinian children to hate tourists and other Western influences was more powerful than anything he could say. Those trips certainly gave me a different perspective on life, and especially on those who are in need.

On New Year's Eve in 1981, we were staying at a hotel in Jerusalem, and he called me up to his room. On some of our trips, he would give me a history lesson or a sermon about some obscure biblical point, so it wasn't entirely unusual for him to call me over. But with it being New Year's Eve, I didn't know what to expect. Before I even had a chance to sit down, he started tapping his fingernails on the bedside table—a habit that he would employ on car windows, church pews, desks, and any other solid surface he could find.

"The word *gap* appears only once in the Bible," he said.

"Okay . . . ," I replied. *Where in the world is this going?*

There was a pause as I waited for him to tell me the point, but he only repeated himself.

"The word *gap* is mentioned only once in the Bible."

Then he said, "Now, you run along and have fun, and don't stay out too late."

That was it! He had summoned me up to his room for a ten-word sermon. Of course, thirty-six years later, I still remember the verse and the context, and now I have an idea why that word was so important to him. He found it in Ezekiel 22:30: "I searched for a man among them who would build up the wall and stand in the gap before Me for the land, so that I would not destroy it; but I found no one."[10]

Knowing Mr. Littlejohn as I did, I believe it was his way of saying, "I know you're only seventeen years old. And I know this won't seem relevant now. But when you're a man, you may remember New Year's Eve in Jerusalem, when I pulled you away from a party for this short sermon about a man willing to stand in the gap. And maybe then you'll understand: Sometimes God is looking for just one person. One person who is willing to do something different or differently. From that one person, others may draw their inspiration or feel emboldened to stand alongside you."

I don't think I've ever been that one person, but at least I've been aware that it's possible, and even laudable, to be alone and still do what the Lord wants you to do. Most of my heroes in life have stood alone, either in accomplishing their mission or in at least attempting something important. I believe those ten brief words were Mr. Littlejohn's way of saying, "Son, it's okay to stand alone for a good cause."

I'll be honest: I don't remember any other sermon or Sunday school lesson from thirty-six years ago. But I do remember that one-sentence lesson about a single word in the Bible. As quirky as it may seem, that was Dick Littlejohn.

Mr. Littlejohn took me on trips to the mountains of North Carolina and Virginia. He took me to New York, Denver, and Texas. I saw parts of the world I never would have seen apart from my friendship with him. What began as a Sunday school experience turned into a life experience that lasted until the day he died. Actually, it continues to this very moment. Mr. Littlejohn's mentoring of me affects every facet of my life—from how I view Democrats to the complexity and composition of my faith, and even to my marriage to the most beautiful woman I've ever met.

When I left for college at Baylor in 1982, I had just met Terri, who is now my wife. Those were the days before texting and e-mails, so our only choices were regular mail, which took several days, or long-distance landline phone calls, which were very expensive. Mr. Littlejohn knew how beautiful and sweet Terri was, and that my chances of keeping her were *de minimis* if I went to Texas while she stayed in South Carolina. So he gave me a phone card and said, "Son, I expect you to call her every day." Heaven knows what those daily phone calls cost him, but he believed in the value of relationships, and whatever he spent on that phone card was worth it to him. However, he did wonder aloud on more than one occasion—as many people still do—how I was able to date such a gorgeous, sweet, talented, smart woman, let alone marry her. I was happy to abide the ridicule, as long as Mr. Littlejohn kept those phone cards coming.

In some ways, Mr. Littlejohn was like a grandparent, except he never put me on restriction, and he was free to minimize whatever mistakes I made. Plenty of times, I tested the limits of his patience—getting lost in Tanzania while he was on a bus to Ethiopia leaps to mind—but his response was always the same: "Son, I love you. I have heard worse than whatever you are about to tell me, and it's all going to be just fine." And you know what? It always was just fine. He showed me what grace looked like. It didn't matter what I had done. I could have told him that I had just robbed six banks and I'd stolen a car to do it, and he'd say, "Listen, son, I've heard worse." I'm sure he hadn't, but that's what he would say.

In terms of unconditional positive regard, he was a lot like my mom. She has always been my fiercest ally and defender. She's the one who sent me extra money in college after my father's lessons in austerity did not quite take hold with me. She is what moms are—the first to love us, the last to love us, and the one who loves us the most in between. But parents have to love you, don't they? When someone else holds you in such high regard, it feels different and unexpected.

Mr. Littlejohn was a lifelong Democrat, and he was one of the most racially progressive and racially complicated men I've ever known. I never heard him utter a racially insensitive word. He consistently hired and promoted people of color, and he gave men like Red Dawkins, Bunny Clowney, and James Betsill opportunities for professional and personal success because he saw them as men—not as black men. He hired a black manager for a store in an affluent, predominantly white neighborhood, because "that young man deserved a chance to succeed."

During the summers of my college years, he hired me as one of only a handful of whites working in a tobacco warehouse. That was his way of saying, "You are going to have relationships with people who are not the sons of doctors."

Our view of God is shaped by different sources in our lives. It could be our parents, a pastor, a teacher, or a friend. My view of God was shaped by a man who never drank alcohol, but who paid for others to go through rehab. My view of God was shaped by a man whose own kids seemed close to perfect, yet he understood and even encouraged the imperfections in other people's kids.

Mr. Littlejohn helped me to understand there are at least two ways to view everything—and oftentimes many more. He was never condescending. He was always positive. He was always comfortable with who he was, and he didn't mind if anyone thought he was eccentric or weird. He had a certain irreverence about him that actually enhanced my faith. In fact, he was the most irreverently reverent man I've ever known. He took himself not-so-seriously in ways that exposed the sanctimony in others. In many respects, he was an enigma, but once you got past the unconventional approach and the quirky intensity of some of the things he said, you were hooked for life.

Mr. Littlejohn lived long enough to see the boy he took to Washington win a seat in Congress, but he didn't live long enough to see me serve. He always told me he wanted lawyers to conduct his funeral, because he wanted it to be a long service—a not-so-subtle jab at the verbosity of lawyers. True to his word, he left instructions to have me preach part of his funeral.

Because of Mr. Littlejohn, I see people as people, not in shades of skin color. Because of him, I know everyone has the same hopes, dreams, and aspirations, but not always the same opportunities. Because of him, I try to treat the poorest of the poor with dignity. I learned from Mr. Littlejohn that if you're going to help people, help them quietly so they can retain their dignity. Because of Mr. Littlejohn, I felt compassion for both the mother of the victim and the mother of the defendant after I finished a murder trial.

"Anyone can show compassion for the innocent," he would say. "Jesus was compassionate even to those who did wrong."

He was totally at peace with who he was. He always saw the other side of the argument, but he never wanted to argue in the first place. He personified the biblical virtues of love, forgiveness, and charity, packaged with a streak of rebellious good humor and a disdain for false piety. From Mr. Littlejohn, I learned unconditional love and extravagant grace. He went to his reward in 2010, but his voice still rings in my mind.

Whatever it is, we can fix it.

I've heard worse than what you're going to tell me.

We can find a way around this.

I remember he always carried his mail tucked inside the front of his dress shirt. I have never seen it done before or since—other than when my wife points out that I do it too. No suit he wore ever fit; they were always too big. His hair was usually a wreck, and he constantly chewed on breath mints. Wittingly or unwittingly, I turned out a lot like him. My suits don't fit, my hair is an unmitigated disaster, and I've been known to carry a pocketful of Life Savers. Those are some small ways in which I grew up to be like him. But it's the larger ways he shaped my life that made him the single most powerful influence I've ever had, apart from my own family.

My parents separated when I was about seven years old, and their divorce was my greatest sadness for a long time. I can still remember sitting on the couch in our home on an Air Force base in Michigan, wearing my winter coat, bawling, and trying to figure out how to keep my family together.

Can we stay together if I don't need any birthday presents?

How about if I give up my Christmas list?

I would have done anything to keep my parents together, to keep our family intact. But of course I couldn't fix it. When the time came, we left my dad behind, went back to Charleston, and moved in with my grandparents. My mom, my brother, and I shared a bedroom for the next two years. My mother worked as a nurse's aide, changing bedsheets and bedpans. She did the lowest-level stuff, just above the custodial staff. It was a meager lifestyle for a very long time, but she never gave up. After the divorce, she had to work longer hours, including night shifts and double shifts, but she was unwilling to let us fall through the cracks of a broken home. She always said, "Shoot for the moon. If you miss, you'll land among the stars." My mother trained me up in the way I should go. She believed the best, and she required it as well.

My mother, Frances, had a proverbial master's degree in the science of discipline, and my grandmother had a full PhD. My brother and I grew up with a firm understanding of what I call *the psychology of the switch*: the task of going out to the tree to choose your own instrument of punishment.

(You might think a larger switch would be more painful, but the truth is, the smaller switch moves faster and hurts more. Believe me, I'm an expert.) Today, people might frown on her style of discipline, but I'm forever thankful that my mother and grandmother cared enough to discipline me.

I believe the real child abuse, however, is allowing your kid to grow up on his own and follow his own authority until he ends up incarcerated. Real child abuse is when a parent ignores the responsibilities of discipline. That kind of neglect continues to cost our society in terms of human potential, not to mention the toll it has taken on individual lives. It's important to create boundaries for your children, to celebrate good behavior and punish bad behavior. I learned it at home from my grandmother and my mother—two women who would not allow me to fail. My mother switched me only a few times in my life, but a couple of those times were in the ninth grade, when I was on the verge of flunking out of school.

During my freshman year, I began to drift. Looking back, I can see that all drifting leads in the wrong direction. My report cards dating back to third grade said that I was a nice boy, but too talkative. I soon discovered that I could draw attention to myself by being the class clown. It wasn't always positive attention—especially from my teachers—but I was hungry for it. I knew that my mother loved me, but I wanted to be noticed outside our home as well.

I had teachers who expected a lot from me, and that didn't mesh well with my primary goal of getting attention.

I remember that my freshman English teacher was an especially tough cookie. She wanted me to do well, and she wasn't willing to cut me any slack or give me any options for extra credit. When I couldn't negotiate my way out of a D in her class, I thought she was the meanest person on earth. But English wasn't the only class where I had trouble. I outright failed Spanish, world geography, and civics. (I may be the only US senator who didn't pass civics—which proves that God has a sense of humor.)

In all honesty, I didn't feel that bad about failing. It was a little embarrassing, sure, but I could take it in stride. My mother, on the other hand, would have none of it. She was not about to have her son become a statistic. She promptly enrolled me in summer school, and I clearly recall that she made me pay for it myself. It was not a fun summer for me, and she was absolutely okay with my degree of discomfort. I worked my tail off to catch up with my classmates, but emotionally speaking, I was off course and I didn't know the way back.

I got a job at the movie theater inside Northwoods Mall in North Charleston. Unfortunately, in those days, there was only one movie per theater. *An Officer and a Gentleman* played for twenty-seven weeks in a row. Then *Return of the Jedi* played for . . . actually, I think it may still be playing at that theater. They paid us just enough so we didn't quit, and we worked just enough so they wouldn't fire us. There was free popcorn, free drinks, and unlimited free viewings of *Star Wars*.

There was a Chick-fil-A in that same mall. I would visit as often as I could, and I would wait in the longest line because there was a very cute girl behind the counter. I always bought just the waffle fries because I couldn't afford the chicken sandwich. (I still highly recommend those waffle fries.)

John Moniz was the guy who ran the Chick-fil-A. Over time, he noticed that I kept showing up at the counter and ordering small waffle fries and a water. During that same time period, his two grade-school-age sons often came down to play at the movie theater. (Picture kids eating excessive amounts of popcorn and rolling each other around in giant trash cans.) I think he started to wonder about this young man his kids were hanging out with.

One day, Mr. Moniz made his way down to the theater during one of my slower shifts, and he brought a bag of Chick-fil-A with him—with large fries *and* a sandwich. He slid it across the concession stand counter and just started talking to me about life. He didn't stop by every week, or even very often, but over time a mentoring relationship began to develop in a most organic way. And it all started when he just came by to say hello and brought me some Chick-fil-A. (Don't miss that part.)

John Moniz came along at just the right time. After flunking out of freshman year, I was trying to get my life back on track, but I was looking for something I didn't know how to find. Fortunately, my mother continued to believe in me and hold me accountable, and my grandmother was a true prayer warrior. For years, she had been praying my head above water. John Moniz was an answer to her prayers, and he began to work on my heart. He had no ulterior motive. I just knew that he believed in my potential.

I don't recall that he ever quoted any Scripture, or even talked to me much about the Bible, but his spirit resonated with me and his success was so impressive. Back in the 1980s, Chick-fil-A gave a new Lincoln Continental to their top store operators, and John earned one of them. I remember watching him drive past and thinking, *Wow, I wonder what you have to do to get one of those!*

I remember that we talked about what was possible. He was able to answer so many of the questions I had about succeeding in life. I was pretty good at football, and I had my eye on the NFL, thinking it was the only possible path out of poverty. He appreciated my athleticism, but he told me I needed a backup plan, and he encouraged me to pursue all my options. He reminded me that I needed an education if I wanted to learn the skills I would need to achieve my full potential. He taught me about being a business owner, not just an employee. He taught me that having a job is a good thing, but *creating* jobs is better. He showed me that making an income is a really good objective, but earning a profit is how you create real wealth. He encouraged me to realize that I could have a good life and enjoy myself, but I could also become a leader and help others. Starting with simple conversations, he planted seeds that began to germinate.

I needed good teachers who could help me learn how to listen more than I talk. I needed someone to model leadership for me, to show me how it could be done. John Moniz was so important to me because he showed me a world of possibility. He introduced me to motivational speakers such as Zig Ziglar and Jim Rohn. Their approach is philosophical and inspirational, but it basically comes down to enlightened self-interest. I learned that it is in my best interest to help someone else before I look for someone to help me. I learned that even a poor kid with no financial resources could make a substantial difference in the lives around him. John shared those motivational tapes with me, and anyone who knew me could see how the trajectory of my life began to change. With my desire to be liked, I learned how to win favor with others by being happy and offering encouragement. I became the most dependable kid in my senior class (even if I still always ran a few minutes late). I became the guy who listened to people's problems, who analyzed their options with them and helped them to find a solution. Sometime during my junior or senior year, I began to believe that all things were truly possible. My grades were now solid, and my leadership skills continued to blossom.

It's impossible to measure the impact that John Moniz had on the way I saw the world, but it's clear that who I am today is due in part to the significant contribution he made by being the right person at the right time in my life. In part because of his influence, I became an entrepreneur, and my financial life changed. Even more important, I have been able to reinvest the lessons he taught me into thousands of other lives. I have also had the opportunity to share some of my memories with his sons, who were too young to understand some of his more powerful lessons before he died. Even during the difficult times when race played an oversized role and was a negative influence in my life, I had memories of a man who gave unselfishly, with no real expectation of a return on his investment, who encouraged me that God can use each of us to have a positive impact on others.

I met John Moniz when he was thirty-four years old. He died from a pulmonary embolism when he was thirty-eight. I often say that the last four years of his life were the first four years of mine. The truth is, we all need someone to model the expectation and show us the way. Leadership is caught, not taught. If you don't have a good model at home, look for one outside your home. If you have the wisdom that comes with experience, find someone younger and share what you've learned. John Moniz went out of his way to become a mentor to me, and it made all the difference in my life. Along with the inspiration and instruction, the faith and love I have always received from my mom, I am what I am today in part because of what John Moniz invested in me. We can all do that for someone.

Every boy wants his father's approval, but only some boys get it. When Jesus was baptized in the Jordan River, he came up from the water, and God said, "This is my beloved Son, in whom I am well pleased."[11] That is the anointing that every man is looking for. Part of the dysfunction in our society today stems from the mass numbers of young men who need that kind of approval and aren't getting it. It's one thing to father a child; it's something else entirely to *be* a father to that child. It's our fathers who launch us into manhood.

From inner-city violence to drugs in the suburbs to the divorce rate nationwide, one reason our country has gone off course is because so many kids today are growing up without their dads in the home.[12] More than one out of four kids in America are being raised in a household without their dads. That number increases significantly in the black community, and we have no way of knowing how many kids are growing up with a father who is present in body but absent in soul, spirit, and positive influence.

To highlight the importance of fathers is not to disparage the efforts of all those single moms who are doing their best to cover both roles for their kids. But I don't think anyone would argue in favor of a single-parent household as the ideal. We need *both* parents. We need our dads every bit as much as we need our moms. And vice versa. That's how we were created. That's how we're designed.

All around us, we see the ramifications of boys and girls who are looking for a complete and balanced view of who they are—and settling for an incomplete version of themselves. For so many kids growing up today, the compass is broken. But before we can solve the problem, we have to understand it. The problem is not our schools; schools play a role in our social development, but they can't compare to the family. In a society without dads, restoring the family is a bit like putting Humpty Dumpty together again. But that doesn't mean we're hopeless and without options. Mentoring can begin to fill the gap and restore the lost leadership. Mentors can change the game, re-chart the course, and alter the outcome in every way. I've seen how it can happen in my own life.

I love my dad, and our relationship has healed a lot throughout my lifetime. But my mom is my hero. Because of John Moniz's inspiration, example, and encouragement to become a business owner, I have been able to provide a better life for my mom. Now I feel as if I am living her American Dream. She set me on the right path, and I had mentors and teachers along the way who kept me on it.

When I went into politics, my mom was surprised. She said, "I think it's time for you to go into ministry."

"I think so too," I said. And then I added, "Ministry in politics."

My mother and I initially disagreed over whether or not I would be able to share my faith in my political office. But we both agreed that there is no better place for me to serve than where God has placed me.

10

Let's Talk about Solutions

Where We Go from Here

TIM

Sometimes our history seems much more powerful than our present circumstances. We can feel as if we are weighed down by the burdens of past decades, past generations, or past relationships. In order to focus on the bridges we're trying to build, we must be willing to forgive what others have done—or not done.

I tell Trey he has the burden of a good memory, because he remembers *everything*. At first, he didn't understand why I would call it a *burden*, because it seemed that having a good memory would be a positive thing. It helps in school, it helps in politics, and it certainly helps when you're playing games like Trivial Pursuit. But it doesn't necessarily help when you're trying to clear a path toward reconciliation. Memory can become a burden when you can so easily recall the bad things that have happened, the ways in which you have felt wronged, or the ways you have suffered.

I grew up playing football, and one thing I learned was not to dwell on previous mistakes. When you make an error, the best thing you can do for yourself and for your team is to let the play end when it ends. Start the next play with a clean slate. You can't be worried about the missed block or the missed cut to the outside that would have allowed you to score. If you're still thinking about the last play, you're bound to get clobbered on the next one. Having a short memory with the challenges of the past can serve us well because it allows us to get on to the next opportunity. That isn't to say we forget about the past, but we learn from it and keep moving forward.

A powerful way I've learned to clean the slate is by remembering how much I've been forgiven. I need to take responsibility for my own actions and attitudes before I start looking at anyone else. I can't blame the white guy or the black guy, or "that woman" or "that man." That's the wrong place to start. The honest truth is that the slate that most needs cleaning is the one inside each of us—the one that has all our preconceptions, prejudices, and poisonous attitudes written on it. The one where we have recorded all our pain. When I look in the mirror and see someone who has been forgiven, it's easier for me to clean the slate with others and start fresh.

Reconciliation can never begin with *me* telling *you* to clean your slate. It begins with me telling you about the struggles I've had trying to clean my own slate. I'll admit it's hard to do when there's some history—when you've been repeatedly stopped by the police for Driving While Black. Or if you've been the recipient of racial slurs. Or if you've experienced segregation and isolation in college. Or if you have suffered from childhood experiences that remain with you into adulthood, even though you've done your best to rise above your circumstances. Nobody said that cleaning the slate would be easy; but I hope you'll be able to see that cleaning the slate is possible, and even desirable.

How do we clean the slate if we're the ones who feel victimized? Sometimes it's helpful to consciously set aside the struggle and try to see things from the other side, to see what might have been the intention of those who caused you pain. I have found it very helpful to assume that the other person's intentions were good—or at least not evil or malicious. Even if what happened was painful, the person's intentions may not have been bad. And if the intentions were good, it leaves enough margin for the two of you to work together to reach an understanding. When I have approached people who have wounded me, or people who have made me mad, I find that my interpretation of their actions is often very different from their intentions. That leaves a wide-open door for reconciliation, restoration, and understanding.

I have to start with me. You have to start with you. We must begin with an honest assessment of our own attitudes and actions.

TREY

As Tim and I have gotten to know each other, I've learned about some things that happened to him in the past, before we ever met. Tim could have used his history as a plausible partition between us in our friendship, but he has never once imputed the actions of others to me. He masterfully realizes that the past is a huge obstacle to throw in the way of any current friendship.

If we want to establish friendships with people who are different from us, we simply cannot blame them for the things that others have said or done to us in the past. We cannot afford to blur the lines of responsibility. We must believe the best about each other and give each other the benefit of the doubt. In a sense, we are all living with the consequences of what others have done or not done, but let's not attribute those things to one another. Let's make an intentional decision to start fresh.

Tim and I have had different life experiences, including our interactions with law enforcement, how we're treated in public in the course of our daily lives, how the media treat us, and the feedback we receive on our various Twitter feeds and Facebook pages. Tim's experience includes things I would *never* be exposed to, and I've had circumstances in my life that he would not readily relate to. So let's be crystal clear: Cleaning the slate is incredibly difficult to do. Fresh starts are always challenging. New beginnings must be intentional and mutual. They require restraint, grace, and love. If we're going to move in the direction of reconciliation, we should not blame each other for what other people have done. Although it's impossible to forget the past, we can choose not to *dwell* on it. We can make a conscious and deliberate decision to forgive others and ourselves.

TIM

I once heard somebody say that the windshield on a car is so big compared to the rearview mirror because it's more important to look forward into the future than back into the past. Sometimes it seems as if our nation is weighed down by all the anger, injustice, and pain of the past. That's too much for *anyone* to bear.

Cleaning the slate does not mean minimizing, excusing, or forgetting the past. Our history matters—both how we got here collectively as a nation, and how we move forward into the future—but when we clean the slate, we make a conscious decision to allow the past to remain in the past. We don't dredge it up and make it foundational in our present relationships. It isn't that we don't remember, but we choose not to allow the past to impinge on our present relationships. I make a deliberate and conscious decision not to charge *you* with the responsibility of repairing the past. You weren't there, it wasn't your fault, and you can't change what has happened. I can't make you responsible for the words or actions of others who crossed my path before you. What I *can* do is have a conversation with you about the friendship we're building together here and now. Later, after we have established a foundation of trust and understanding, we can give each other permission to dig deeper and delve into challenging areas.

If we really want to make a difference, let's have a conversation—just you and me. Let's not talk about the weight of the world or the weight of the past, but let's talk about where we are right now. Let's start with a clean slate; let's assume the best of each other and *expect* the best of each other. Let's give each other the benefit of the doubt. Let's build our rapport and establish credibility and trust with each other, and then we can share what we've learned, and share our victories with others who can then do the same.

TREY

When I think about problem-solving across lines of division, the word that comes to mind is *intentionality*. Unlikely friendships don't just happen. To be successful, they must become a priority. We have to make time for them on the schedule. I'm convinced most of the world is walking around in circles looking for a friend. If we would just be still for a moment, someone who is also looking for a friend is bound to bump into us. When we develop friendships with people who differ from us, we don't have to become godparents to each other's children, and we don't have to go on family vacations together. But if we can establish a certain regularity and intentionality to our relationship—a primacy that says the relationship is important enough to make time for one another—we can accomplish a lot with people we might otherwise think we have little in common with.

There are members of the House with whom I may *never* share a common vote, but many of them have children the same ages as mine, some are former prosecutors, some share my love for sports, and we all love this country—and that's enough to form the basis of a friendship, even if our voting cards are different in every way. Simply put, most of us have most things in common, so let's focus on *that*.

<hr />

TIM

One thing I've noticed during my time in Congress is that members who differ on particular issues may try to come up with policy proposals and legislative remedies without first agreeing with their opponents on the nature of the problem they're trying to solve. So it's no surprise when they can't reach a bipartisan agreement on their proposed legislation.

This happens not only in politics. It can be an obstacle to cooperation and problem-solving anytime people with differences try to work together. So how do we go about defining a common problem that we can solve together?

One thing Trey and I have wrestled with over the years is how to have a productive conversation about racial reconciliation—as if there were a way to simply talk about it and find a solution. What we've discovered is that the road to reconciliation is paved with *understanding*—that is, being able to see the situation from the other's perspective.

Sometimes the easiest way to solve a problem together is *not* to attack it head-on and try to figure out a solution. When two people who are very different are at odds with one another, sometimes the best first step in working toward a solution is to defuse the tension by catching a movie together, sharing a meal, or doing some social things together. We may not find that the problem completely goes away, but the emotional *intensity* that can preclude us from working together on a solution oftentimes will ease, allowing the answer to manifest itself.

It may sound basic, but Trey and I have found that understanding and reconciliation often start with food. The simple act of sharing a meal can break down barriers and create a climate of cooperation. We use the opportunity of breaking bread together to talk through some of the problems and challenges we face, and maybe discuss some of our differences. Not to overplay the analogy, but food reminds us of our common humanity and our need for nourishment and refreshment. If the medium is the message, then sitting down together over a meal says, "Whatever our differences, we're in this together, so let's work it out."

Food may be a good mediator, but it's no substitute for rapport, credibility, and trust. Problem-solving will be more effective when we've taken the time to establish strong relationships first. When we've already invested in building friendships, we're better able to identify problems from a common perspective. Even if we disagree on the best solution, we can work our way toward a mutually acceptable and beneficial outcome by starting from a place of basic agreement.

TREY

Here's the truth: Most of us in this world want the exact same things for ourselves and our families. We all want to live in peace, freedom, and harmony. We want the opportunity to earn a living doing meaningful work for a fair wage. We want time with our loved ones, and the health to enjoy it. And we want our children to grow up with the same opportunities. So why can't we focus on everything we have in common, build honest relationships based on mutual interests, and work together to find solutions for the problems and challenges we all face?

I'll be honest: I'm tired of all the division. I'm tired of the disunity. I'm tired of people who manufacture reasons to fight. I want us all to be able to see a world that consists of only two kinds of people. Not black and white, not Republican and Democrat, not gay and straight, not rich and poor, not male and female. But rather, people of good conscience and people who are not of good conscience. When you boil it all down, that may be the only true difference of any significance.

My dad used to say that if God had a sense of humor, he would put certain people next to each other in heaven, particularly people who did not get along on earth. I'm not sure about the theology, but I get his point: Eternity is a long time to carry a grudge.

My maternal grandmother, Jessie Lee Evans, and Tim's maternal grandfather, Artis Ware, never met in this life. But they would have enjoyed each other. They both grew up poor, and not far from one another, in the same region of South Carolina. They both worked hard and were devoutly religious. Of course, they never would have gotten to know each other in the South Carolina where they grew up. In those days, blacks and whites didn't go to school together, worship together, or do much of anything together. It was a segregated society, and that segregation contributed to the way they viewed the world.

Their grandsons, however, grew up in a different South Carolina. One where we can not only go to school together, but we can teach a class together. And we do! One where we can not only eat together in a restaurant, but we can actually eat all of our dinners together in Washington, DC, as we do. One where we can not only run for the same offices, but explicitly choose to run together—campaigning together, doing media together, and even debating our opponents together.

South Carolina is different today, and my friendship with Tim is living proof of that. But we can do more—in South Carolina and across this great land. We can be more fully reconciled across all lines of division. The story of race relations in America is an analogy for other divisions that still exist within our society today.

We live in a world that prioritizes diversity over unity, but let's stop for a moment to recognize that those terms are not mutually exclusive. We can be unified *within* our diversity. We can allow our diversity to bring wisdom, texture, and depth to our unity. We have so much in common, and I don't know why we don't spend at least as much time talking about our commonality as we do our differences.

I didn't grow up in a segregated world, and I cannot imagine living in one either. We're all missing out on one of the greatest blessings of life if we don't pursue a friendship with someone who grew up differently from how we did, who doesn't look like us, who doesn't think like us, but who wants the same things from life that we do. All we have to do is just sit down and listen. Seek to understand a different perspective. Find points of agreement and harmony. Build rapport, credibility, and trust.

Let me make this personal. If you will seek to establish an unlikely friendship with someone who differs from you, I promise you that one of two things will happen. Either you will see things from a new perspective that you've never considered before, and you will be changed; or you will become even more convinced, after careful reflection, that your approach to life is right and proper. Either way, you win.

Even if you decide that your own beliefs are correct, that doesn't necessarily make the other person wrong. And once you've seen life through a different set of lenses, you'll understand better how a person of good conscience could reach conclusions different from your own. And maybe—just maybe—you'll find a way to move forward together, building bridges of cooperation and understanding as you pursue mutually beneficial outcomes.

You have nothing to lose by trying.

Let me give you an example.

My brother-in-law, Britt Dillard, is a minister in South Carolina. He's a wonderful person who always has a positive word of encouragement for everyone he meets. So I wasn't surprised to hear that he greeted and encouraged a young black man he met at a fast-food restaurant around Christmastime one year.

"Take care, brother," he said as he picked up his order and prepared to leave.

"No disrespect, sir," came the quick retort, "but we are not brothers."

At this point, my brother-in-law had a choice. He could continue on his way to the door and avoid any potential escalation in the dialogue. He could be defensive, since he meant no offense by what he said. Or he could recalibrate and see if this might become a small moment of reconciliation. True to his character and his deeply held spiritual beliefs, Britt chose the latter, riskier option—to see if a bridge, however small, could be built.

"Oh, I don't know about that," he replied. "If you believe

in God, we are brothers. If you're going to celebrate the birth of his Son in a couple of weeks, we are brothers."

By offering a gentle and conciliatory response, Britt opened a window of opportunity. He and the young man spent the next thirty minutes finding out that they actually had a lot of things in common. Truth is, we all do.

We're not going to solve the great complexities of life the first time we meet someone. But we can start building a foundation by listening. We can start by trying to understand. It may not feel natural at first, and it may even be terribly awkward. But try reaching out to someone who does not expect it. Simply say, "I'd like to have a conversation. I'd like to get to know you, and I'd like to understand your perspective. I'll let you choose what we'll talk about. We're not going to argue, we won't correct each other, we won't rebuke each other, and we won't try to talk over one another. My main purpose will be to listen. And let's see where we go from there."

TIM

About twenty years ago, a white pastor, Wendell Estep of First Baptist Church of Columbia, South Carolina, and a black pastor, Charles B. Jackson Sr. of Brookland Baptist in West Columbia, became friends at the local gym. Soon they were working out together every Monday, and they attended the National Prayer Breakfast together in Washington, DC. Through the course of getting to know each other, they

soon discovered that they held many values in common—
not the least of which was their common faith, which led
them, informed them, and challenged them. Before long,
they became interested in working together as friends, not
just hanging out at the gym together.

In 2000, believing that Christians who trust in the resur-
rection of Jesus Christ should celebrate together, they held
a joint Easter service at Williams-Brice Stadium, with more
than thirty thousand people—both black and white—in
attendance.

In 2003, they held an event called America 2003, with
about twenty thousand in attendance at a service to honor
our military during the Iraq War. The Columbia Urban
League asked Reverend Jackson to speak and Pastor Estep
to introduce him.

Both men know that their relationship is real because it
took time to develop. The process of forming friendships
across lines of division requires us to come face-to-face with
our own past, our own feelings, and our own previously
held beliefs, and then to come face-to-face with, and seek to
understand, others who have a different past, different feelings, and different beliefs. Reverend Jackson and Pastor Estep
discovered that once you know someone wants to reach the
same destination, it is much easier to trust them with the
steering wheel. That commonality of purpose, that shared
desire for reconciliation and unity, is enough to get things
started. The key is getting to know each other personally, not
as part of some sort of program, but in a real relationship.

Both pastors are old enough to remember a time when their relationship would have been improbable, if not completely unimaginable.

In the spirit of reconciliation fostered by Pastor Estep and Reverend Jackson, our hope is to inspire other white and black church groups to come together in combined Bible studies on the topic of racial reconciliation. From our experience with the Pastor/Police Roundtables, bipartisan efforts on Capitol Hill, and successful community initiatives at all levels, we hope to foster personal relationships between people who might not otherwise get together, and to do it in a confidential and safe environment that promotes honesty, civility, understanding, and community.

Unlikely friendships will create waves in our communities. When we're willing to reach across lines of division and focus on what we have in common, not on what separates us, our actions will affect people more than we realize. We need to decide what kind of waves we want our friendships to make.

Years ago, Senator James Lankford and I started something called Solution Sundays, where we encourage people who are not like each other to have a meal together—and not just at a restaurant, but inviting others into our own homes. The inspiration for this came when James started asking his friends, "When was the last time you had a person of a different race in your home?" He was surprised to learn that many of his friends and people from his church had never had a person of a different race in their home. One way we've found to identify a common problem to address with people we might otherwise not agree with is to break bread together.

Family is the most basic subunit of culture, and friendship is probably next. These relationships are what enable us to identify problems and work toward solutions. But if we're surrounded solely by people who think exactly as we think, then our friendships become merely a series of ratifications of our own viewpoint. We're never challenged or stretched.

I love hearing different people's perspectives. Even if I don't enjoy it at the time, I find that I benefit from hearing how other people view the same set of facts, the same circumstances, or the same challenges. To a certain extent, we're all prisoners of our own backgrounds—of the way we were brought up, the opportunities we've had or the setbacks we've faced, and the experiences we've collected along the way. So when we intentionally align ourselves with people from different backgrounds and with different perspectives on life, we open ourselves up to an entirely new world.

Even in something as divisive as politics, in an environment where people don't agree on much of anything, you'll find some remarkably strong across-the-aisle friendships. It's a sad reflection on where we are as a culture that we so often feel inhibited in saying that publicly. I count Joey Kennedy,

Tulsi Gabbard, Kyrsten Sinema, Cedric Richmond, John Yarmuth, and Hakeem Jeffries, among others, as friends. All are Democrats. Some might find it surprising that we could be friends, and there are others who might even be angry about it. *How could he? How could he be friends with someone like that?* The answer is really pretty simple. Most of us have most of life in common. We want the same things. We just disagree on how to get there. So, what are we going to focus on? The parts where we disagree or the fact that we want the same things? We've chosen to build rapport, credibility, and trust with one another, and we seek to understand our various viewpoints as we work toward solutions that will benefit everyone. We choose not to allow our differences to separate us from our common goals.

TIM

After the Charlottesville protests that resulted in the deaths of Heather Heyer and Virginia state troopers Berke Bates and Jay Cullen, we saw a remarkable response in South Carolina when leaders of the Black Nationalist Movement and the South Carolina Secessionist Party held a joint press conference in support of their common goal to make sure there would be no violence in our state in response.[13] Here you had folks who want to lead a new revolt to secede coming together with folks who are the antithesis of everything they stand for—the Black Nationalist Movement—because both parties saw *violence* as the real problem and their groups as part of the solution.

When I saw this, it gave me real hope. If you can bring a white secessionist together with a black nationalist in the city where the first shots of the Civil War were fired, because they both love this state enough that they're willing to work together to solve the underlying problem of racially motivated violence, then *all things* are possible.

TREY

Not long after Tim and I were elected to the House of Representatives, he taught me an important lesson about how we should respond to people who oppose us. I think it's also a good first step whenever we want to reach across lines of division to establish relationships with people who may not be charitable toward us at first.

In those early days in Washington, we both spent too much time reading comments and criticism on the Internet and social media. It's probably unavoidable at first. You don't want to miss a question, or a comment, or a criticism. You eventually learn not to be terribly concerned with what someone who has never met you thinks about you; but when you are brand new to politics, you probably obsess a little too much. So when a writer in South Carolina wrote a gratuitously nasty blog post about Tim, I was infuriated.

Anyone can have a voice on the Internet or through social

media, and I'm just fine with that. If you want to criticize a vote, have at it. If you want to critique a policy position, take your best shot. But this post crossed the line in its attack on Tim's character, and I was very upset on his behalf.

Now, if it happened today, everything would be different. I would not have read the blog in the first place. If I did, I probably wouldn't go down to Tim's office. I wouldn't distract him with such nonsense. I would stay quiet and hope he hadn't seen the article. But when you are brand new and don't know any better, you read and react.

Tim's office back then was one floor below mine in the Longworth House Office Building. So I hurried down the stairs, walked past his receptionist, and went straight into his office.

"Have you read this?" I said.

I can't recall now if he had, but it didn't take long for me to brief him on the content. I said, "I'm sick of this. It's time to do something about it. It's difficult for a public official to seek legal redress over defamation, but something must be done."

"You're right," he said. "Please close the door and have a seat."

I thought, *Now we're making some progress. I finally got Tim Scott fired up enough to respond.*

I closed the door, and Tim said, "We're going to pray for this person."

"No, I'm not," I said. I don't typically pray out loud anyway, and I certainly wasn't about to start then. "You can, but

I'm not." You have to be pretty angry to refuse to pray with someone. But I wanted action, not a prayer.

Tim shrugged and said, "Well, will you sit with me while I pray?"

So I sat with him. And I listened as he prayed for someone who had written words that were intentionally calculated to be hurtful. He prayed earnestly for this man who had tried to defame him, who had treated him like the enemy.

Without making a point of it with me, Tim simply modeled what Jesus teaches: "Love your enemies and pray for those who persecute you."[14] But he didn't pray where others could hear it and say what a great guy Tim Scott is. He prayed behind closed doors with earnestness and fervor like he was praying for good health for a dear friend. The contrast was not lost on me. I was not the victim, but I was angry. Tim was the victim, but he forgave and prayed for the person who had wronged him.

Tim has never told this story, and he doesn't love it when I tell it for him. He doesn't think he was doing anything unusual or special. He was just doing what the Good Lord commanded him to do. But I was there. I heard him do exactly what we are commanded to do—pray for our enemies—and I heard him do it with a gentle spirit and a genuine beseeching for God's movement in this person's life.

Tim is one who lives out his faith, who literally prays for his enemies—if he even thinks of them as his enemies, which he probably doesn't. I'm a little more like Peter, the disciple of Jesus who was quick to pull out his sword and fight—the guy who took off another guy's ear, but only because he missed his neck.

I learned some valuable lessons through this experience:

- Don't read and react to Internet articles.
- If you want to retaliate against someone for causing harm, don't talk to Tim Scott about it. He'll wind up humbling you with his faith.
- Most important: If you want to break down the walls of division between yourself and other people, start with prayer. Prayer as a first option is always a good place to start—even if you don't pray out loud with other people.

TIM

For people of faith, prayer is always a good place to start. The Bible tells us that "the weapons we fight with are not the weapons of the world. On the contrary, they have divine power to demolish strongholds."[15] Prayer is certainly foremost among those weapons. Through prayer, we call on God to change people's hearts and minds—not so they'll agree with us, but so their intentions and actions will be brought into alignment with what *God* desires. We can pray the same for ourselves—and we should.

One thing that Trey and I have seen up close and personal during our time in Washington is that you can't expect people who have sharp ideological differences on matters of conscience to set those differences aside in order to reach a political consensus. That's why we have elections. But it's important to realize, as we contemplate the divisions in our society, that most people we meet are people of good conscience with honest differences. And the issues we face are rarely cut-and-dried. For example, there was a time in history when people believed the world was flat. With more information and exploration, this was proven untrue. In the same way, there are many subjects on which we may disagree profoundly, but with more information and exploration, we may discover we are not quite so polarized in our views.

So, for me, it's not so much about how we vote, but how we frame the other side's intentions on most issues. Unfortunately, in our increasingly polarized, 24/7 news environment, opponents are often vilified and their motives called into question. Moreover, *compromise* has become the word to avoid. Within the Republican Party, we're often led to believe that we are either committed to the cause or a RINO* or a sellout. But how can we expect to bridge a fifty-fifty ideological split in the country through power politics? If there's a lesson to be learned from the past decade, it is the futility of such an approach.

The first steps in the direction of understanding and reconciliation are exactly the steps we've been discussing here: reach out to people of good conscience whose views differ

---

* Republican In Name Only

from our own; pursue genuine friendships by building rapport, expecting the best, giving the benefit of the doubt, and building credibility and trust. Only then can we reasonably work together to agree on what the problems are and work together toward solutions.

If half the country wants a single-payer health care system and the other half wants a totally private system, neither side is going to get everything they want. We've already seen what happens when one side musters enough votes to push something through. But can we not agree that we both want essentially the same thing: healthy citizens and affordable costs? And as we work together toward a solution that does the least harm and the most good, can we not be respectful in how we frame the other side's position?

When the mob came to arrest Jesus, and Peter cut off the ear of the high priest's servant, Jesus healed the man's ear.[16] That's how he handled his enemies. But too often we don't seek restoration amid the chaos. Some politicians run negative ads that misrepresent the other side's views, because winning is all that matters. Rather than plotting and planning for the next election, why don't we make good governance the goal? Why don't we recognize that we're all in this together and come to the table as people of good conscience dedicated to the welfare of all our citizens? Unless we put down our swords and seek to understand, trust, and work with those who differ from us, there's no chapter that can be written on how to reconcile a fifty-fifty split—on any subject.

When Trey and I first undertook this project, we agreed

that we didn't want to write a political book. That's a tough challenge for two members of Congress, but we didn't want to get off track talking about political differences in Washington, DC, and risk having our readers miss the essential point—that friendship, honest dialogue, and working together toward reconciliation and restoration are the keys to solving our differences in *any* arena, regardless of what those differences might be. We've touched on some seemingly intractable issues—if race and politics don't get you stirred up, let's add religion to the mix—but there's a lot of ground to be taken, much that can be redeemed and restored, and strides of progress to be made as we work together in good faith to reconcile our differences and become one nation under God, indivisible, with liberty and justice for all.

True friendship is born out of unconditional love and acceptance. The Bible is very clear that love is not simply an emotion; it is a deliberate commitment. Love and acceptance are not situational. They're not contingent. They are consistent. I'm very optimistic about our future, but if we're going to change the world, it's going to happen one relationship at a time. It's going to happen by all of us enlarging our comfort zones to make room for unlikely friendships—friendships with people who, at first glance, it may appear we have little in common with. But just as love is unconditional, it is also intentional. We must decide to look beyond our differences to build bridges of commonality. Pursuing unlikely friendships will require us to do things that seem uncomfortable at first.

But what's hard gets easier, and if we'll do the hard things first, we will soon reap the benefits.

TREY

Like Tim, I believe that friendship has the best chance of transforming our world. We can legislate and make people conform their conduct, but no piece of legislation can change someone's heart. Years ago, they passed a law that said that people like Tim and me could go to school together. But they couldn't pass a law that said we had to be friends with each other.

As a former prosecutor, and now a legislator, I can tell you there's a time and a place for conforming people's conduct. But how great would it be if our motivation didn't come from a rule, a regulation, or a law, but instead from discovering we have more in common with other people than we have differences?

I think we will find that to be true, if we will take the time to hear each other out. There will be some rocky points, issues on which we strongly disagree even after we've listened to the other side, but if we make an intentional decision to be friends no matter what, then we can get through anything. We'll both be stronger for the effort. There's no law that can make people care about each other. That desire must come from someplace else. To me, that "someplace else" is friendship.

Epilogue

Hope Is the Agent of Change

TIM

The key to reconciliation is living life together. Trey and I can talk about race because we also talk about the Dallas Cowboys. We can talk about hard, honest things because I honor his wife and he calls my mother on her birthday. We focus on what we have in common—which is pivotal if you're going to build rapport with someone. It's everything we have in common that allows us to gravitate toward conversations about problems and opportunities. Talking about the simple things in life increases credibility and opens a pathway to the more difficult conversations. Building on a foundation of trust gives us permission to delve into topics that we wouldn't necessarily discuss at the dinner table on Thanksgiving or Christmas. But in order to get there, we had to invest the time, build a genuine rapport, and establish a lot of credibility.

Clearly, we don't choose our friends for the purpose of gaining influence or accomplishing some great goal. You can't start there. If you end up working together to solve a common problem or make a positive difference in some area, that will come later, after your bond of friendship is secure. Still, I believe it can happen. I am confident that the future of our nation and the world hinges on people of good faith acting in good ways.

I have hope for our country in part because of what has happened in South Carolina between my grandfather's generation and my own. Over the past fifty years or so, we have emerged from an Old South that was segregated, divided, and filled with challenges into a place so transformed that my grandfather could never have imagined it when he was a younger man.

My grandfather, Artis Ware, was born in Salley, South Carolina, in 1921, at a time when the look of a man determined his potential. Like many other black children at the time, he dropped out of elementary school to work in the fields and pick cotton. He never learned to read. I remember listening to him talk about his experiences of having to step off the sidewalk whenever white folks came along. He learned early in life never to look a white person in the eye.

Eventually, as South Carolina began to change, he got

a job at the Port of Charleston. And though the job didn't give our family much in the way of tangible resources, it kept a roof over our heads. My grandfather worked hard, my mother worked sixteen-hour days, and they sacrificed over and over and over to share the lessons they learned. They made sure that the future would be brighter for my brother and me than it was for them.

Over the course of my grandfather's lifetime, everything changed for us. Racial attitudes, though still not perfect, have come a long way. Opportunities my grandfather never had are now available to me and to future generations. And the values of hard work and self-reliance have taken us all to a higher level. That's the beauty and strength of America.

In my own experience, I have seen the power of unity in diversity. Every Thanksgiving and Christmas, my home is filled with life and laughter as I enjoy the holidays with a diverse collection of family and friends—my good friend who led me to the Lord, along with his wife and daughter, all of whom are white; my high school friend Mikel, who is a law enforcement officer and whose daughters are biracial; and of course my own family, who are black and Korean. Together we celebrate life and all that we have in common.

Trey and I are both optimistic and encouraged about the future of our country. Our optimism is rooted in our common faith in God and in his promise to guide us and sustain us as we trust in him. We're optimistic because we have seen so much good in people of diverse backgrounds. We have hope because we have seen a remarkable spirit of inclusiveness in the younger generations. Even though our nation may seem divided on the surface, we have confidence that we can get better as a people.

This is our vision for the future of America. We believe that our nation can be unified and transformed by conversations and friendships that lead to reconciliation and understanding. As Americans, we must uphold the ideals of freedom, equality, justice, and opportunity, even as we continue to work together to make those ideals a reality for all. We must come together, find solutions, and get to a point where we can see that our strength as a nation is rooted in all that is good in our world.

Acknowledgments

TIM

I have always said that I have the best friends in the world. Their loyalty, encouragement, integrity, and compassion are indeed rare, and I am truly blessed. Thank you for entering my life, for shaping my story, and for lighting my path.

My mother deserves all my gratitude for her unfailing belief in her children. She not only believed we could reach for the stars, she expected us to.

My staff and colleagues are the finest group I could imagine, and our work is both challenging and rewarding. Their partnership makes the celebrations doubly enjoyable and cuts the burdens in half. I am thankful to belong to a team so dedicated to excellence.

TREY

My parents provided me with the best beginning a child can have: a loving environment, all of life's necessities met or exceeded, an appreciation for education, a spiritual foundation, a great example to follow, a chance at a better life than they had, and a good name. I also have three sisters, who remain dear to my heart. I always thought I wanted a brother until I realized how having three sisters prepared me even better for life. So, thank you to my first family, for a childhood and upbringing that most children would give anything to have.

To the sweetest, most beautiful, and most Christlike person I have ever known: my wife, Terri. She is vastly more talented than her husband, but she ordered her life to allow me to pursue my dream of being a prosecutor because I wanted to make the world a better place. Because she is so disciplined and talented, she also managed to find time to take care of our precious children, go back to school to earn a master's degree and become certified to teach, and become a first grade schoolteacher. And she has been a perfect mom to our two children, Watson and Abigail, the joys of our life.

To the women and men I have worked with in the US Attorney's office, the 7th Circuit Solicitor's office, and our congressional office: Thank you for your hard work and dedication to a better world. You epitomize public service.

To all the teachers I've had through the years: *thank you*. Teaching is the most important form of public service. I wish I had realized that truth earlier in life. Thank you for your sacrifices. Thank you for your patience. Thank you for controlling your surprise that I would ever read a book, much less write one. And thank you for all the times you did not call my parents, when you said you would.

Finally, to all the people over the course of the last twenty years who have offered me encouragement and accountability. I include people I have known since I was a kid, who give me their perspective at the grocery store every Saturday morning, and I include the people who speak to me at airports all across the country, who challenge me with their constructive criticism. One must keep the encouragement and the criticism in perspective, in hopes of finding the essential life balance called self-awareness. For the past twenty years—and especially during my time in Congress—people have been far kinder to me than I deserve, and they have been more measured in their criticism than I could expect. I thank you for both.

Finally, thank you to Frances Scott. This book was supposed to be about your son Tim and your family. It was supposed to be about *your* hard work, *your* faith, and *your* determination that your children would turn out as well as they did. But you raised a son too modest to write a book about himself. Maybe one day we can convince him to do that.

TIM AND TREY

Greg Johnson, with WordServe Literary Agency, thank you for representing our work in the publishing world.

Tricia Heyer and Janet Thoma, thank you for your partnership, unfailing optimism, and occasional pushes! Janet helped us get off the ground (with help from our longtime friend and former colleague Sue Myrick), and she has kept us on task ever since. We met Tricia as a result of something she wrote about her late husband. Trey was on a plane, sitting between two strangers—which is not the time to start crying as you read about two people you've never met. But eventually we met Tricia and she helped us put into words what was in our hearts. She did it with constant encouragement and unconditional positive regard—which, as two members of the nation's least popular group, we were not accustomed to.

We have rich and rewarding friendships with many of our colleagues—on both sides of the aisle. But once we mention one colleague's name, we had better be prepared to list them all. So, for fear of leaving anyone out, we will just say thank you to all our friends who are also our colleagues. You have added depth, texture, joy, and accountability to our lives.

Still, we would be remiss if we failed to offer a special thank you to our friend Kevin McCarthy. He was one of the first friends we made back in 2010, and he has been consistently good to us ever since—from the floor of the House to a corner table in a quiet restaurant; when everyone can see it and when no one is there to notice. Kevin has helped us both personally and professionally, and always with no expectation of anything in return. Kevin, you are the same gregarious, kind person in public and in private. Thank you for being a friend far more than even a colleague. Thank you for all that you do for us and for others—bestowing gifts of guidance and encouragement for which you seek no credit or attention.

Notes

1. Jennifer Steinhauer, "Hoping for a Senate Seat, the Friendliest of Rivals," *New York Times*, December 13, 2012, www.nytimes.com/2012/12/14/us /politics/trey-gowdy-and-tim-scott-senate-aspirants-and-friendliest-of-rivals .html.
2. Luke 10:30-35
3. Jeff Hartsell, "'A Lot of God, a Little Bit of Me,' Says Chris Singleton, Son of Emanuel AME Victim, on Being Drafted by the Chicago Cubs," Charleston (SC) *Post and Courier*, June 14, 2017, www.postandcourier .com/sports/a-lot-of-god-a-little-bit-of-me-says/article_62970240-512a -11e7-85ee-43768f82249c.html. We encourage you to take a few minutes to watch the video embedded in this story of Chris Singleton, son of Charleston shooting victim Sharonda Coleman-Singleton, speaking to the media on the day after his mother's death. As tragic as the circumstances were for this young man, his responses to the reporters' questions are inspiring.
4. Emily Badger, "Political Migration: A New Business of Moving Out to Fit In," *New York Times*, August 16, 2017, www.nytimes.com/2017/08/16 /upshot/political-migration-a-new-business-of-moving-out-to-fit-in.html.
5. Stephen R. Covey, *The 7 Habits of Highly Effective People* (New York: Fireside, 1990), 235–260.
6. "Direction of Country," RealClear Politics, www.realclearpolitics.com /epolls/other/direction_of_country-902.html, accessed September 11, 2017; "The Disunited States of America," interview with Scott Keeter, director of survey research at the Pew Research Center in Washington, DC, *Reflections*, Fall 2012, http://reflections.yale.edu/article/who-are-we -american-values-revisited/disunited-states-america.

7. 1 Samuel 19:1-7; 20:1-42
8. Proverbs 27:17
9. See Proverbs 27:17; Ecclesiastes 10:10; Hebrews 4:12.
10. NASB
11. Matthew 3:17, KJV
12. "Living Arrangements of Children under 18 Years and Marital Status of Parents, by Age, Sex, Race, and Hispanic Origin and Selected Characteristics of the Child for All Children: 2014," US Census Bureau, 2015, Washington, DC, www.census.gov/data/tables/2014/demo/families /cps-2014.html. Numbers cited include children "living with mother only" and children "living with neither parent."
13. Rebecca Shapiro, "A Secessionist and a Black Nationalist Join Forces after Charlottesville," *HuffPost*, August 18, 2017, www.huffingtonpost.com/entry /a-secessionist-and-a-black-nationalist-join-forces-after-charlottesville_us _59968acfe4b0a2608a6b75a9.
14. Matthew 5:44
15. 2 Corinthians 10:4
16. Luke 22:50-51

About the Authors

Tim Scott is a successful small businessman and US senator from South Carolina. Having grown up in a poor single-parent household, he has made it his mission to positively affect the lives of a billion people through a message of hope and opportunity. He is the first African American to be elected to both the US House and US Senate since Reconstruction, and he currently serves on the Senate Committee on Finance; the Committee on Banking, Housing, and Urban Affairs; and the Committee on Health, Education, Labor, and Pensions.

Trey Gowdy is a former state and federal prosecutor who experienced the criminal justice system firsthand for nearly two decades. In 2010, he was elected to Congress and is now in his fourth term. He is the chair of the House Committee on Oversight and Government Reform and previously chaired the Select Committee on Benghazi. He serves on the

House Permanent Select Committee on Intelligence, as well as the Judiciary and Ethics committees. He has been widely recognized by law enforcement and victims of crime for his diligent service as a prosecutor.

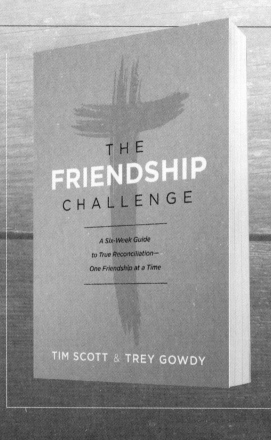

Why Reconciliation?

The Power of Unlikely Friendships

WATCH

To watch the introductory video (3–5 minutes) for session 1, go to the Why Reconciliation? link at www.thefriendship challenge.com.

CONSIDER

Many Americans say they feel disconnected from one another. Why? We are really good at rattling off our differences: liberal or conservative; millennial or baby boomer; black, white, or brown; Catholic or Protestant; Muslim or Christian; one-percenter, middle-class, or poor; Northern or Southern; and the list goes on. In many ways, we are polarized and divided as a nation. But what about our similarities? Can we list those as quickly and easily? How about some of these:

We all want what's best for our children.

We all want to live in a safe and peaceful community.

We all want opportunities for meaningful work that allows us to provide for our families.

We all want to enjoy a nice meal with good company.

We all want a secure future for ourselves, our children, and our parents.

If we think about it, don't we have a lot more in common with other people than we may have realized? Aren't there more things—and more important things—that unite us than separate us? And how many of the things that separate us are the result of different perspectives about how to reach the same goals?

What if, instead of focusing on our differences, we focused on everything we have in common with other people? What if we pursued intentional relationships across lines of division with the goal of reconciliation? What if we formed genuine friendships based on mutual understanding and respect? The point is not to erase our differences—in a pluralistic society, our diversity makes us who we are—but to make an intentional decision to listen, learn, seek understanding, find points of agreement, and disagree with civility and grace. The road to reconciliation begins with a simple choice to invite someone with whom we differ to have a conversation.

REFLECT

1. When have you witnessed the power of a friendship or a relationship to change things for the better—in your family, neighborhood, or community?

2. Think of someone who, at least on the surface, seems totally opposite from you. It may be someone who has opposing views or a different life experience. What makes you different from each other?

   Now describe some of the similarities you have with this same person.

   How does identifying your similarities affect your perspective on your differences?

DIG DEEPER

1. As you read the following passage, look for differences between Jesus and the woman at the well.

Jesus knew the Pharisees had heard that he was baptizing and making more disciples than John (though Jesus himself didn't baptize them—his disciples did). So he left Judea and returned to Galilee.

He had to go through Samaria on the way. Eventually he came to the Samaritan village of Sychar, near the field that Jacob gave to his son Joseph. Jacob's well was there; and Jesus, tired from the long walk, sat wearily beside the well about noontime. Soon a Samaritan woman came to draw water, and Jesus said to her, "Please give me a drink." He was alone at the time because his disciples had gone into the village to buy some food.

The woman was surprised, for Jews refuse to have anything to do with Samaritans. She said to Jesus, "You are a Jew, and I am a Samaritan woman. Why are you asking me for a drink?"

Jesus replied, "If you only knew the gift God has for you and who you are speaking to, you would ask me, and I would give you living water."

"But sir, you don't have a rope or a bucket," she said, "and this well is very deep. Where would you get this living water? And besides, do you think you're greater than our ancestor Jacob, who gave us this well? How can you offer better water than he and his sons and his animals enjoyed?"

Jesus replied, "Anyone who drinks this water will soon become thirsty again. But those who drink the water I give will never be thirsty again. It becomes a fresh, bubbling spring within them, giving them eternal life."

"Please, sir," the woman said, "give me this water! Then I'll never be thirsty again, and I won't have to come here to get water."

"Go and get your husband," Jesus told her.

"I don't have a husband," the woman replied.

Jesus said, "You're right! You don't have a husband—for you have had five husbands, and you aren't even married to the man you're living with now. You certainly spoke the truth!"

"Sir," the woman said, "you must be a prophet. So tell me, why is it that you Jews insist that Jerusalem is the only place of worship, while we Samaritans claim it is here at Mount Gerizim, where our ancestors worshiped?"

Jesus replied, "Believe me, dear woman, the time is coming when it will no longer matter whether you worship the Father on this mountain or in Jerusalem. You Samaritans know very little about the one you worship, while we Jews know all about him, for salvation comes through the Jews. But the time is coming—indeed it's here now—when true worshipers will worship the Father in spirit and in truth. The Father is looking for those who will worship him that way. For God is Spirit, so those who worship him must worship in spirit and in truth."

The woman said, "I know the Messiah is coming—the one who is called Christ. When he comes, he will explain everything to us."

Then Jesus told her, "I Am the Messiah!"

JOHN 4:1-26

a. List at least three differences Jesus had with the woman at the well.

b. How does the woman use these differences to try to avoid Jesus' request for water?

c. What reasons do *you* use for trying to avoid connecting with others who are different from you?

2. Read the next part of the passage:

> Just then his disciples came back. They were shocked
> to find him talking to a woman, but none of them
> had the nerve to ask, "What do you want with her?"
> or "Why are you talking to her?" The woman left her
> water jar beside the well and ran back to the village,
> telling everyone, "Come and see a man who told
> me everything I ever did! Could he possibly be the
> Messiah?" So the people came streaming from the
> village to see him.
>
> Meanwhile, the disciples were urging Jesus,
> "Rabbi, eat something."
>
> But Jesus replied, "I have a kind of food you
> know nothing about."
>
> "Did someone bring him food while we were
> gone?" the disciples asked each other.
>
> Then Jesus explained: "My nourishment comes
> from doing the will of God, who sent me, and from
> finishing his work. You know the saying, 'Four
> months between planting and harvest.' But I say,
> wake up and look around. The fields are already
> ripe for harvest. The harvesters are paid good
> wages, and the fruit they harvest is people brought
> to eternal life. What joy awaits both the planter
> and the harvester alike! You know the saying, 'One
> plants and another harvests.' And it's true. I sent
> you to harvest where you didn't plant; others had

already done the work, and now you will get to
gather the harvest."

JOHN 4:27-38

a. Why were the disciples surprised to find Jesus talking
to the woman?

b. Even though the disciples had witnessed Jesus' work
and mission firsthand, they were still shocked by his
actions. Why do you think this is?

c. Complete the following sentence with the name
of someone with whom you differ: *My friends or
family members would be surprised to see me having
a conversation with* _____. Why would
they be surprised?

d. What is the "nourishment" that Jesus speaks of here? What does he say is the source of this nourishment?

e. Can you say that your own nourishment comes from the same source? Why or why not?

f. If the "fruit" of the harvest is "people brought to eternal life," what opportunities might we be missing if we do not have relationships with people who are different from us?

3. Read the final portion of the passage:

Many Samaritans from the village believed in Jesus because the woman had said, "He told me everything I ever did!" When they came out to see him, they begged him to stay in their village. So he stayed for two days, long enough for many more to hear his message and believe. Then they said

to the woman, "Now we believe, not just because
of what you told us, but because we have heard
him ourselves. Now we know that he is indeed
the Savior of the world."

JOHN 4:39-42

a. Based on these verses, how were the Samaritan
   people affected by Jesus' encounter with the woman
   at the well?

b. What kind of impact could you have on the people
   around you by starting a relationship with someone
   who is different?

c. Are you ready to reach across lines of division in
   your life to connect with someone who is different?
   Explain why or why not, including any hesitations
   or challenges you may have.

RESPOND

1. As Christians, we believe that Jesus reconciles sinners to a sinless God. Moreover, in order to reconcile us to God, Jesus crossed many lines of division. Though he was the Son of God, he was born into this world to an unwed mother, grew up in meager economic circumstances, and had no settled home as an adult. Though he invested his life in helping other people—teaching them the truth about God and about salvation, healing the sick, casting out demons, and restoring people's lives—he was arrested on phony charges, tried before a biased tribunal, and put to death for crimes he did not commit. Even as he was being executed on a cross between two thieves, he cried out to God to forgive the very people who were killing him. His willingness to forgive even the worst of sinners is the foundation for our willingness to be reconciled to one another—even to those who are very different from us, and to those who may even be opposed to us. Jesus' example of sacrificial love is what enables us to offer grace, extend forgiveness, seek understanding, and pursue reconciliation.

   a. How does this perspective affect your decision to initiate a relationship with someone who is different from you?

b. Are there any people in your life who are off-limits? Explain.

2. One of the keys to overcoming problems in our society is finding common ground. We don't have to agree on *everything*, but wherever we *do* agree . . . let's start there. I (Tim) have found commonality to be a powerful tool. Trey understands the concept of mutually beneficial opportunities as well as anyone I have ever met, especially in leadership. His lifestyle reflects what we're talking about. One of the reasons Trey and I have been able to have some frank discussions about problems, challenges, and obstacles—and overcome them very quickly—is that we have intentionally sought to find common ground. No matter what differences we may have with another person—social, racial, political, spiritual, ideological—if we will look for *something* we have in common, or something we can admire or emulate in the other person, we can always build on that.[2]

a. Do you agree or disagree that there is always something we have in common with other people that we can build on? Explain.

b. Why do you think it is sometimes easier to focus on our differences than on what we have in common?

c. Think specifically about the person or group with whom you most need to reconcile. How can starting with common ground open a pathway for frank discussions about problems, challenges, and obstacles?

3. In *Unified*, we discuss our different perspectives on the shootings at Emanuel AME Church in Charleston. Do you recall your first thoughts when you heard about the tragedy? Did you talk about it with anyone? Did the shootings affect you in any way? Why or why not?

4. In Washington, on the day after the shootings, there was a massive prayer vigil on the Capitol grounds. People of every background and political persuasion gathered to pray. It was beautiful and compelling to

see the emotional boundaries lifted, to see people come together to comfort one another. It reminded me (Trey) of all that is *good* about America. But why does it take a tragedy for us to come together so beautifully? Why must we face a calamity before we will join hands, pray, and seek healing?[3]

Discuss your responses to these two questions.

5. I (Tim) have always been impressed by what I call the "aftermath mentality." As Americans, we are so good at treating each other as individuals and family *after* a crisis. Think about 9/11. Think about hurricanes and other natural disasters. It is amazing to see how people will pull together to help, across all barriers and boundaries, when something bad happens. But I would like to see us develop an aftermath mentality *without* the crisis. Maybe we can avoid a future tragedy if we will act like the American family we are without waiting for an *event* to ignite that response.[4]

Discuss your responses to these two questions.

What steps can we take to develop an "aftermath mentality" *before* there is another crisis?

6. How do suffering and tragedy affect our willingness and ability to pursue reconciliation? Do they help or hurt? Explain.

7. How does the kind of forgiveness modeled by the families of the victims of the Charleston shootings factor into reconciliation? What or who needs to be forgiven, corporately or individually, as part of your effort to pursue reconciliation with someone with whom you have differences? In other words, is anything blocking you from pursuing a relationship with someone in the "other camp"?

RECONCILIATION IN ACTION

1. What are some of your own prejudices or fears that you may need to confront and overcome in order to pursue a relationship with someone who is different from you?

2. What steps can you take to start a relationship across a line of separation in your life—an intentional relationship trending toward reconciliation? What are some of the challenges you may face? Who can help you overcome these challenges?

3. Set a date to attend an event that will help you connect and explore reconciliation with someone who is different from you. This is only a first step. You simply want to get out and see how it feels to be with someone from your "other" group as you work to develop further steps to build bridges and find common ground. How could attending a church service or a social function with someone across a line of division help you both begin to reconcile your differences?

4. After the event, write down how you felt. Were you surprised by the meeting? Did you feel awkward, or were you comfortable? How did the person or group receive you? What things did you discover you had in common?